Community

SUCCESS

AN ILLUSTRATED GUIDE TO COMMUNITY ACCESS

Don Bastian

IEP

RESOURCES

Don Bastian, Author
Jo Reynolds, Illustration
Dan Hanson, Editor
Elizabeth Ragsdale, Graphic Design

An Attainment Company Publication
ISBN 1-57861-023-0

Attainment Company, Inc.
P.O. Box 930160 • Verona, Wisconsin 53593-0160 USA
Phone: 800-327-4269 • Fax: 800.942.3865
www.AttainmentCompany.com

Table of Contents

Money Matters 151

Potpourri 159

Appendix 171

Introduction

Community Success is an illustrated encyclopedia of community-based skills. Sixty commonplace activities, like using restrooms, crossing streets and shopping at a department store, are illustrated step by step. Appropriate corresponding social skills are integrated into each activity. For example, when shopping at a department store, students learn communication with store clerks, appropriate handling of store items, when to ask for help and how to return unwanted merchandise.

Community Success encourages independence! Designed primarily for individuals with cognitive or communication disabilities who participate in community-based instruction, the program features clear illustrations and easy-to-find activities. Ideal for low-level readers to use independently.

Community Success follows a four-step process: Review, rehearse, assess and perform.

- First, **review** the activity. Point out the sequence of steps and discuss the problems or issues that can occur during activity performance. Pay special attention to the social "do" and "don't" pictures.

- Then **rehearse** the activity before stepping out. Emphasize steps that the user is having particular difficulty completing.

- **Assess** the user's performance of the activity in actual community situations and establish a goal for skill development. Four Assessment Sheets are provided in the Appendix: Community Success Progress Report, Activity Assessment Sheet, Activity Goals and Routine Goals.

- Finally, help the user **perform** the activity as independently as possible. Use any instructional technique that is effective with the student (modeling, verbal prompts, picture cues) and appropriate for the community setting.

Using these resources, your creativity and the four-step learning process, your students can enjoy Community Success!

At Home

Activity List

Social Skills: Ready to Go
Ready to Go
Social Skills: Answering the Door
Answering the Door
Checking the House
Coming Home

Social Skills: Ready to Go

Allow yourself enough time.

Prepare ahead if possible.

Ask a friend what clothing is appropriate.

Know the weather forecast.

Ready to Go

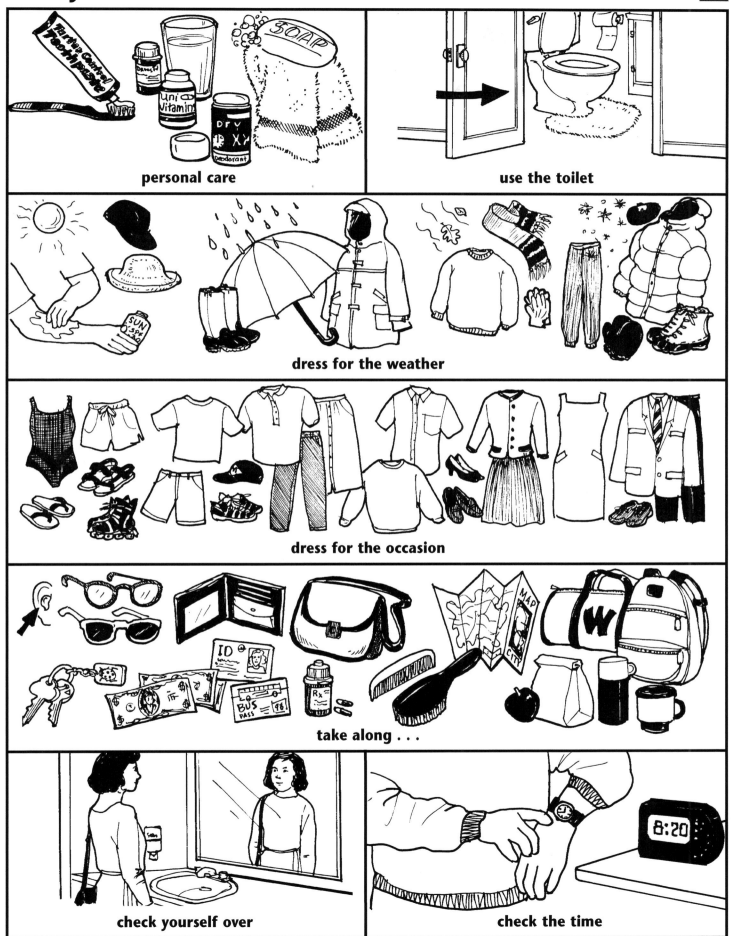

personal care

use the toilet

dress for the weather

dress for the occasion

take along . . .

check yourself over

check the time

Social Skills: Answering the Door

If you're concerned, don't answer the door.

It's OK to say "No thanks."

Control your pets.

Show hospitality to your visitors.

Answering the Door

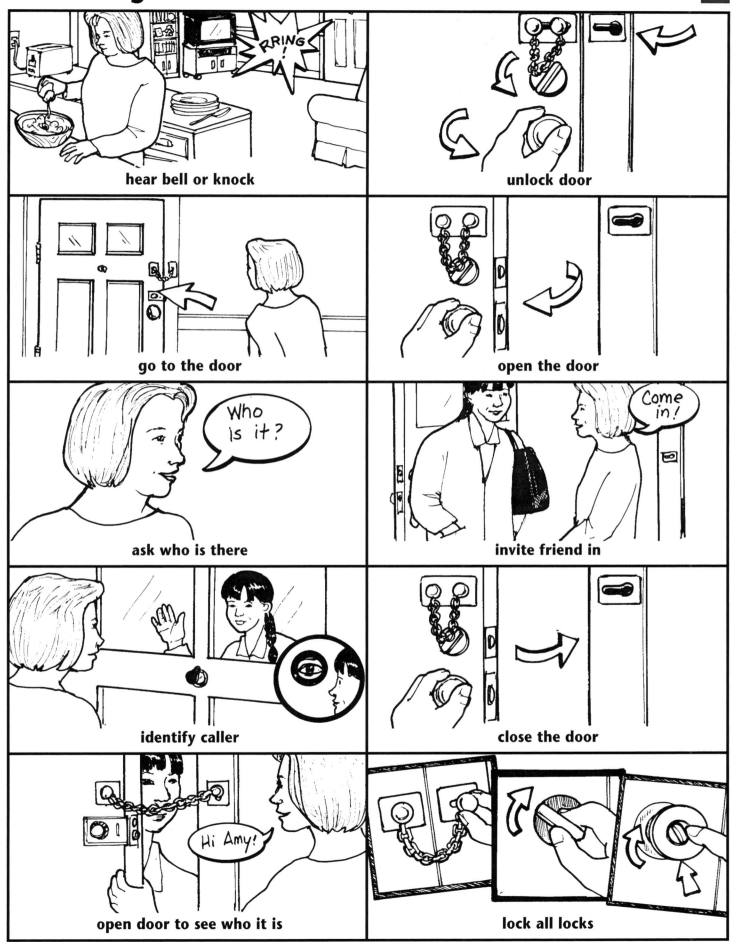

hear bell or knock

unlock door

go to the door

open the door

ask who is there

invite friend in

identify caller

close the door

open door to see who it is

lock all locks

Checking the House

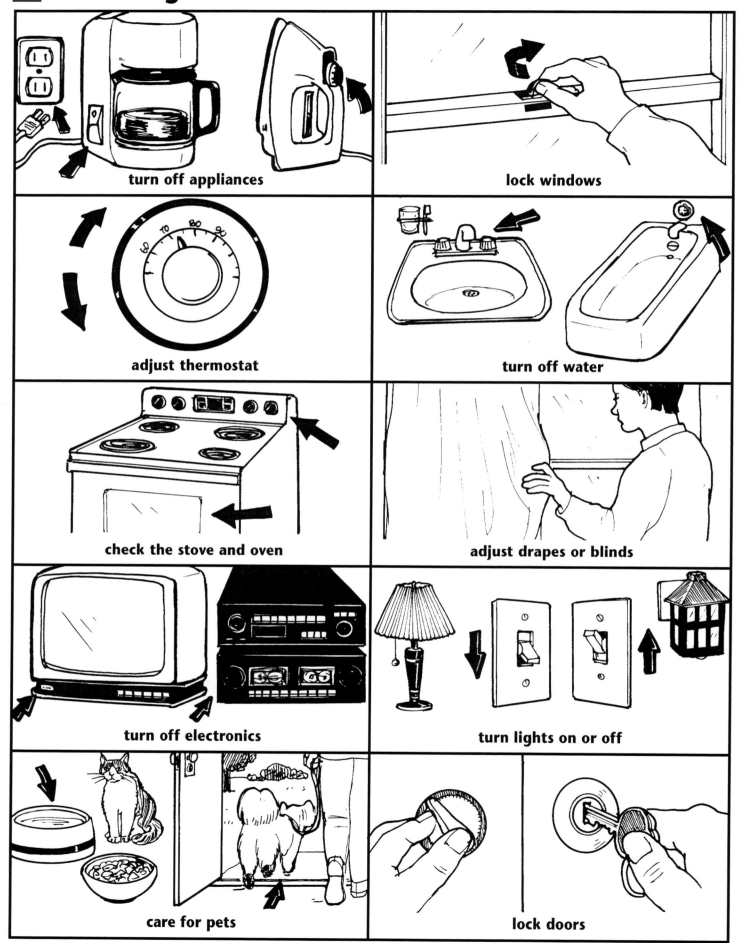

turn off appliances

lock windows

adjust thermostat

turn off water

check the stove and oven

adjust drapes or blinds

turn off electronics

turn lights on or off

care for pets

lock doors

Coming Home

unlock door

unpack

turn the lights on

put personal items away

take your coat off

check mail, newspaper and answering machine

take your shoes off

change clothes

adjust thermostat

care for pets

Any Place

Activity List

General Social Skills
Social Skills: Behavior Tips
Community Places
Stores
Restaurants
Information Signs
Building Access
Social Skills: Men's Restroom
Men's Restroom
Social Skills: Women's Restroom
Women's Restroom
Social Skills: Waiting in Line
Waiting in Line
Asking for Help
Crossing Streets
Social Skills: Walking
Walking
Wheelchair
Social Skills: Elevator
Elevator
Escalator

General Social Skills

Who to talk to

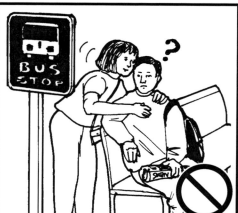

Who to hug or kiss

Who to shake hands with

Who to sit with

General Social Skills

Who to ride with

Who to let in your home

Whose home you enter

Who to flirt, tease or play with

Social Skills: Behavior Tips

Speak clearly, but not too loudly.

Don't stare at strangers.

Don't make rude noises.

Don't make rude noises.

Social Skills: Behavior Tips

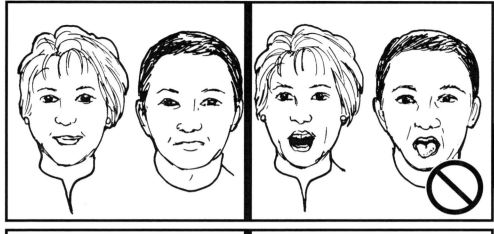

Keep your mouth closed.

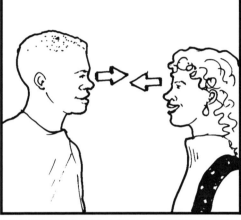 

Look people in the eye when talking.

Use tissues when needed.

Watch what you're doing.

Social Skills: Behavior Tips

Shower or bathe regularly.

Keep your teeth and breath clean.

Keep your hair clean and neat.

Keep your nails and hands clean.

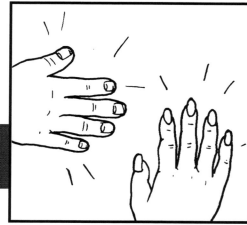
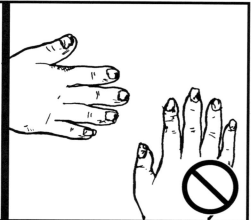

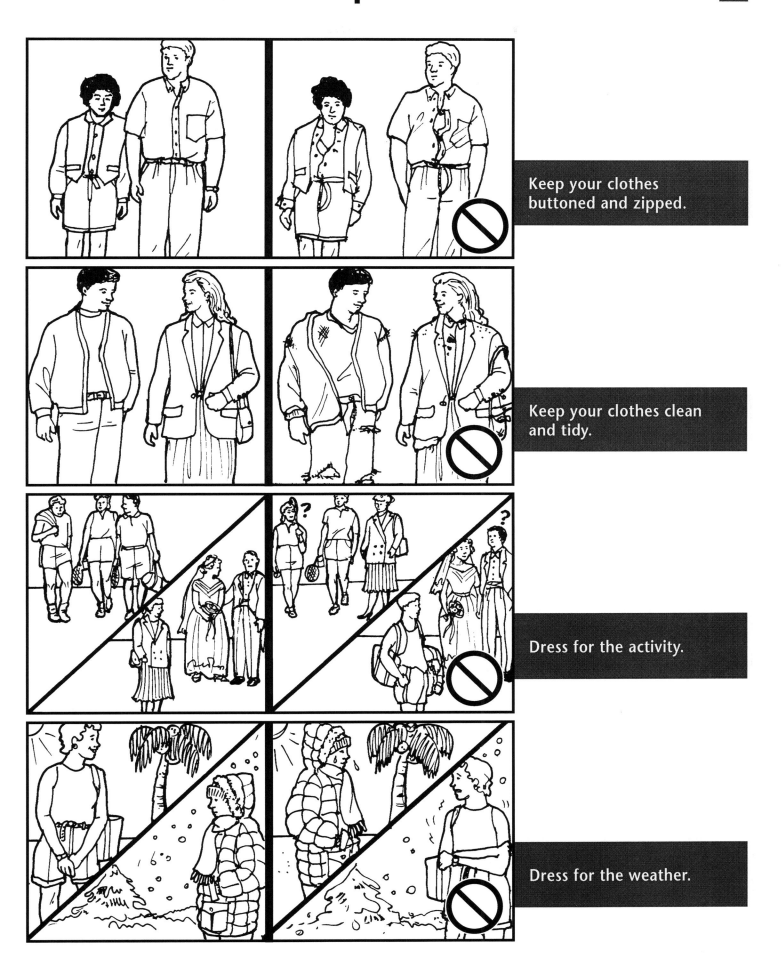

Keep your clothes buttoned and zipped.

Keep your clothes clean and tidy.

Dress for the activity.

Dress for the weather.

house

apartment

school

playground

park

river

lake

beach

restaurant

fast food

Community Places

trailer (park or court)

motel

gas station

hotel

grocery store

department store

bakery

drug store

hardware store

mall

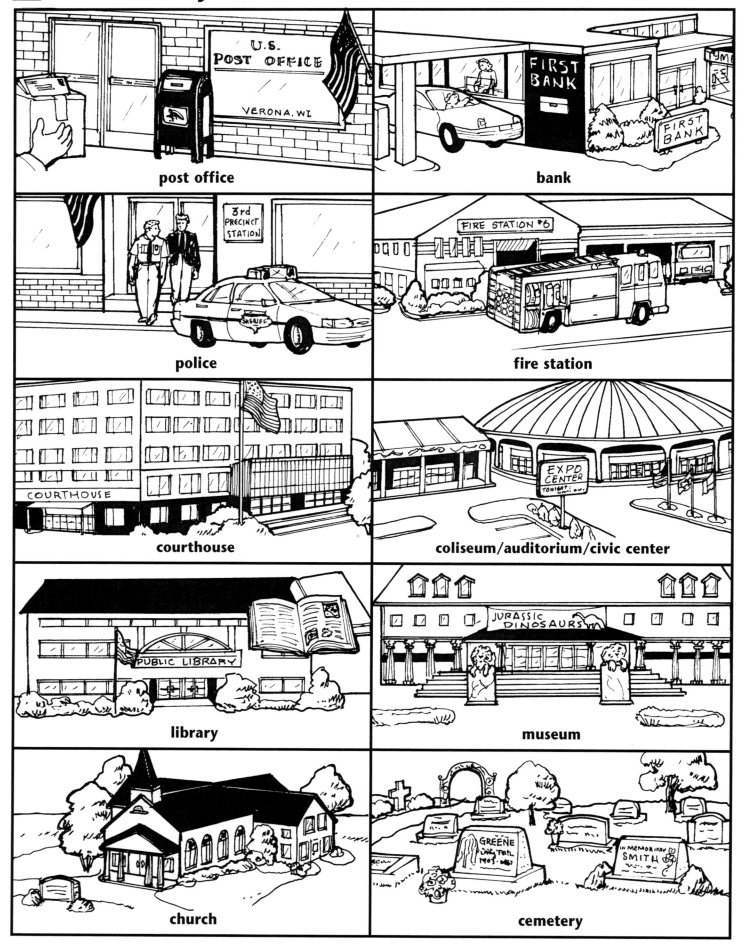

post office

bank

police

fire station

courthouse

coliseum/auditorium/civic center

library

museum

church

cemetery

Community Places

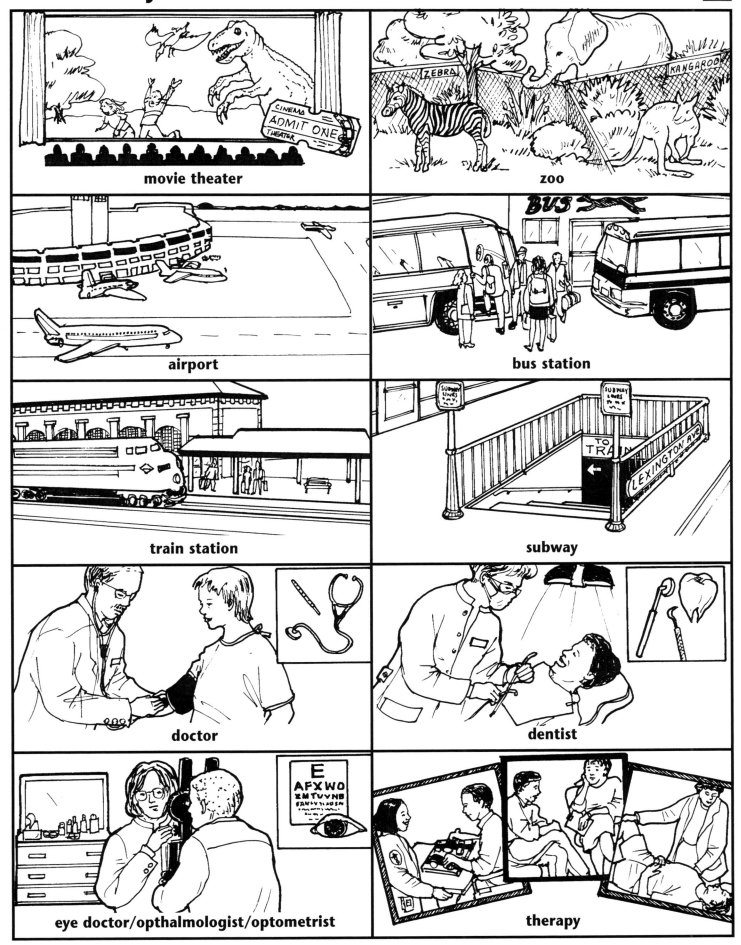

movie theater

zoo

airport

bus station

train station

subway

doctor

dentist

eye doctor/opthalmologist/optometrist

therapy

Community Places

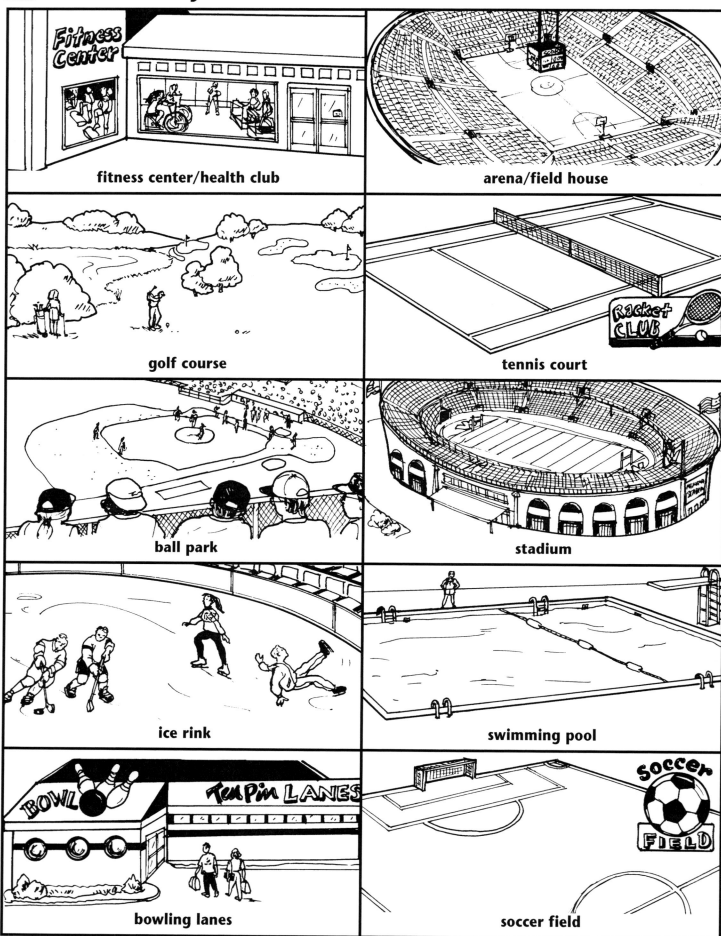

fitness center/health club

arena/field house

golf course

tennis court

ball park

stadium

ice rink

swimming pool

bowling lanes

soccer field

Community Places

laundromat

florist

telephone company

veterinarian

utility company

video arcade

hospital

carnival/fair

funeral home

college

Kmart

Toys 'Я' Us

Wal-Mart

Safeway

Sears

Kroger

JC Penney

Radio Shack

Walgreens

Hallmark

Subway

Kentucky Fried Chicken

McDonald's

IHOP

Denny's

Pizza Hut

Burger King

Wendy's

Hardee's

Taco Bell

walk   pedestrian crossing

danger — keep out

don't walk

no trespassing

bus stop

do not enter

stop

watch your step

railroad crossing

beware of dog

Building Access

enter   do not enter

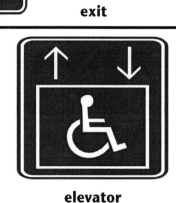

exit

wheelchair ramp

elevator

men's restroom   women's restroom

escalator

telephone

stairway

information

smoking   no smoking

Social Skills: Men's Restroom

Put trash in the correct container.

Respect others' privacy.

Always close your stall door.

Aim carefully.

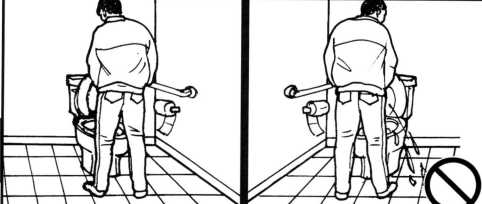

Social Skills: Men's Restroom

Raise the seat before urinating.

Wait your turn.

Check the paper supply when entering a stall.

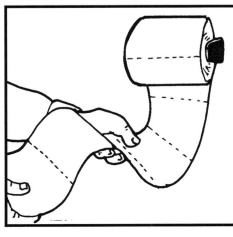 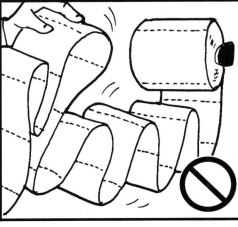

Use the correct amount of paper.

Men's Restroom

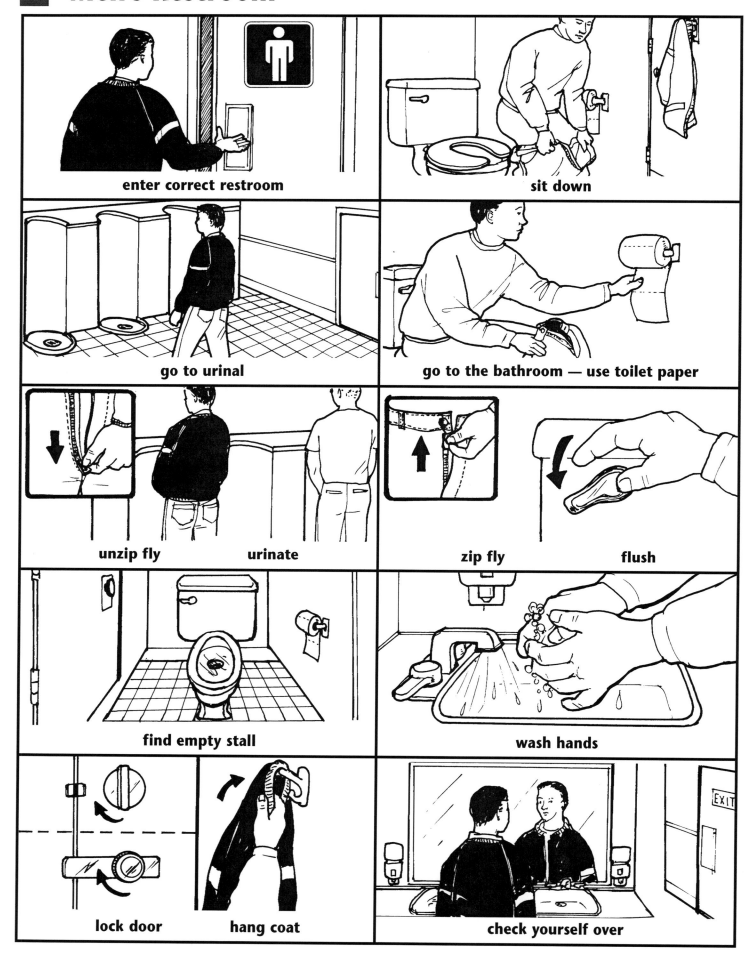

enter correct restroom

sit down

go to urinal

go to the bathroom — use toilet paper

unzip fly   urinate

zip fly   flush

find empty stall

wash hands

lock door   hang coat

check yourself over

Social Skills: Women's Restroom

Check for dry seat before sitting.

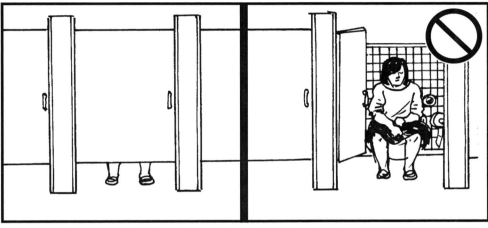

Always close your stall door.

PLEASE DO NOT FLUSH SANITARY PRODUCTS!

TRASH

PLEASE DO NOT FLUSH SANITARY PRODUCTS!

Dispose sanitary items correctly.

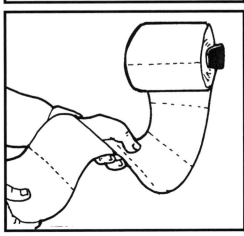

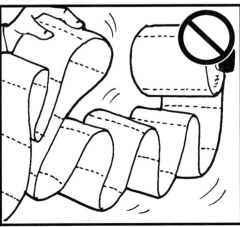

Use the correct amount of paper.

Social Skills: Women's Restroom

Respect others' privacy.

Choose the correct stall.

Wait patiently for your turn.

Check the paper supply.

Women's Restroom

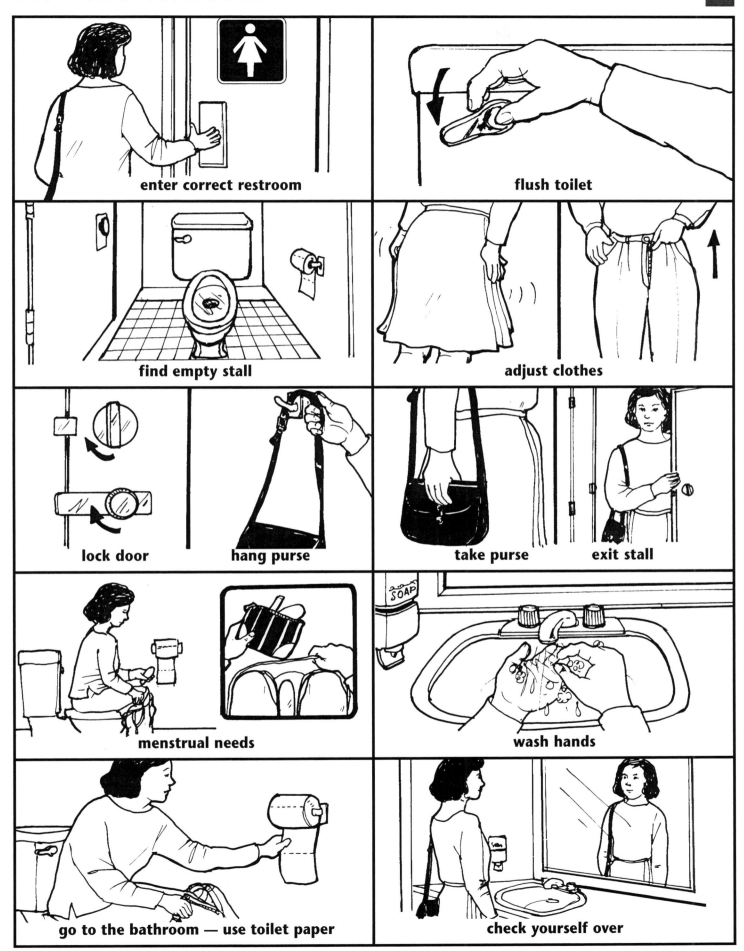

enter correct restroom

flush toilet

find empty stall

adjust clothes

lock door

hang purse

take purse

exit stall

menstrual needs

wash hands

go to the bathroom — use toilet paper

check yourself over

Social Skills: Waiting in Line

Respect others' space and privacy.

Don't cut in line.

Avoid crowding and pushing.

Don't invite others to cut in.

Waiting in Line

go to the end of the line

step forward as line moves

give space to others

wait at counter entrance

wait quietly

wait until clerk is free

protect your belongings

be ready for your turn

wait patiently

your turn

Asking for Help

I've lost my . . .

I need assistance, please

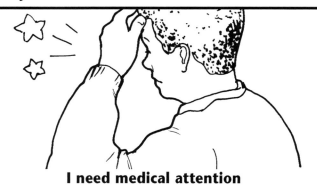

I need medical attention

please call the police

where is the telephone?

I need directions, please

where are the restrooms?

what time is it?

thank you!

Crossing Streets

find crosswalk

stay in crosswalk

push "WALK" button

don't stop in street

wait on "DON'T WALK"

watch for turning cars

cross on "WALK"

don't run

look both ways

yield to emergency vehicles

Social Skills: Walking

Let others pass when you walk with friends.

Give others space — don't follow too closely.

Put trash in waste containers.

Music is not for everyone.

Walking

use map or ask for directions

protect your belongings

use sidewalk

stay in well-lit areas

at night

stay to the right

wear light colors

at night

if no sidewalk, walk facing traffic

stay in busy areas

at night

avoid obstacles and rough surfaces

walk with a friend

at night

Wheelchair

use sidewalk

protect your belongings

stay to the right

stay in well-lit areas

at night

use curb cuts

wear light colors

at night

avoid obstacles and rough surfaces

stay in busy areas

at night

locate accessible entrances

travel with a friend

at night

Social Skills: **Elevator**

Know when it's safe to enter.

Face the front of the elevator.

Know when to press the emergency button.

Say "excuse me" when moving around others.

Elevator

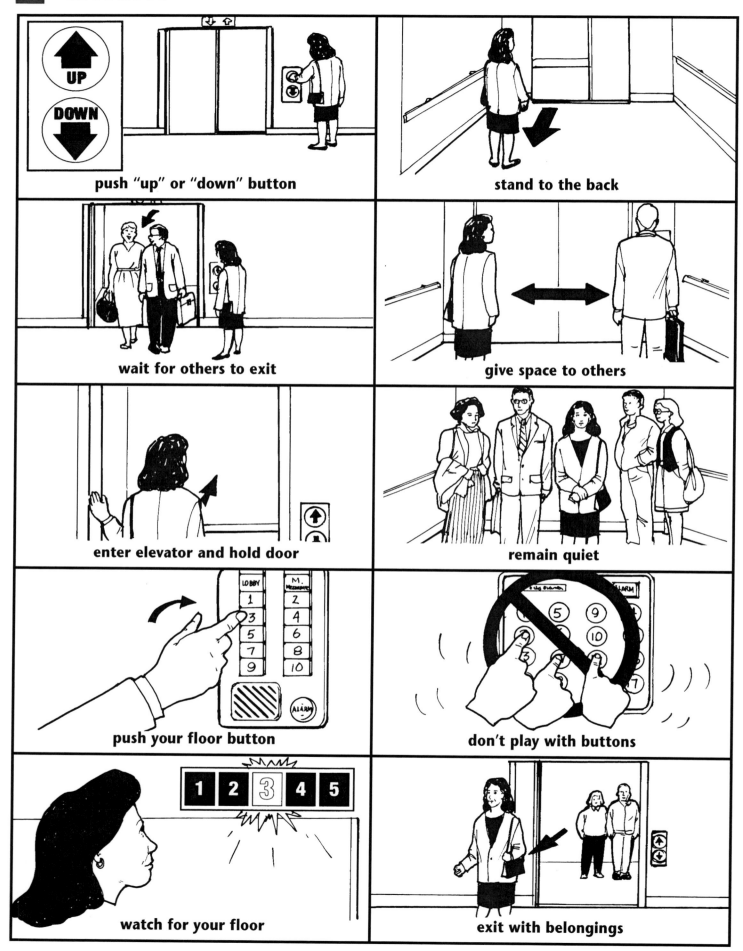

push "up" or "down" button

stand to the back

wait for others to exit

give space to others

enter elevator and hold door

remain quiet

push your floor button

don't play with buttons

watch for your floor

exit with belongings

Escalator

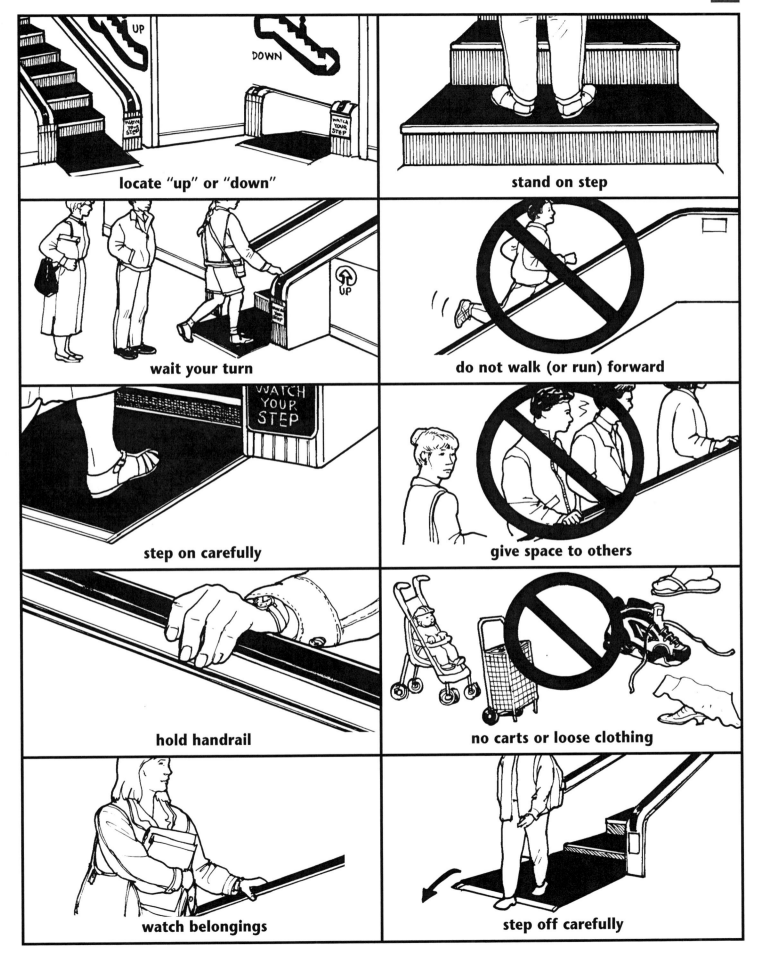

locate "up" or "down"

stand on step

wait your turn

do not walk (or run) forward

step on carefully

give space to others

hold handrail

no carts or loose clothing

watch belongings

step off carefully

Going Places

Community **SUCCESS**

Activity List

Travel Options
Day Trip
Packing Your Bag
Vacation
Social Skills: Hotel — Motel
Hotel — Motel
Car
Gas Station
Social Skills: Bus
Bus
Bicycle
Social Skills: Taxi (Cab)
Taxi (Cab)
Social Skills: Airplane
Airplane
Social Skills: Commuter Train
Commuter Train

walk

school bus

wheelchair

van (ride service)

bike (bicycle)

taxi cab

car

subway train

bus

airplane

Day Trip

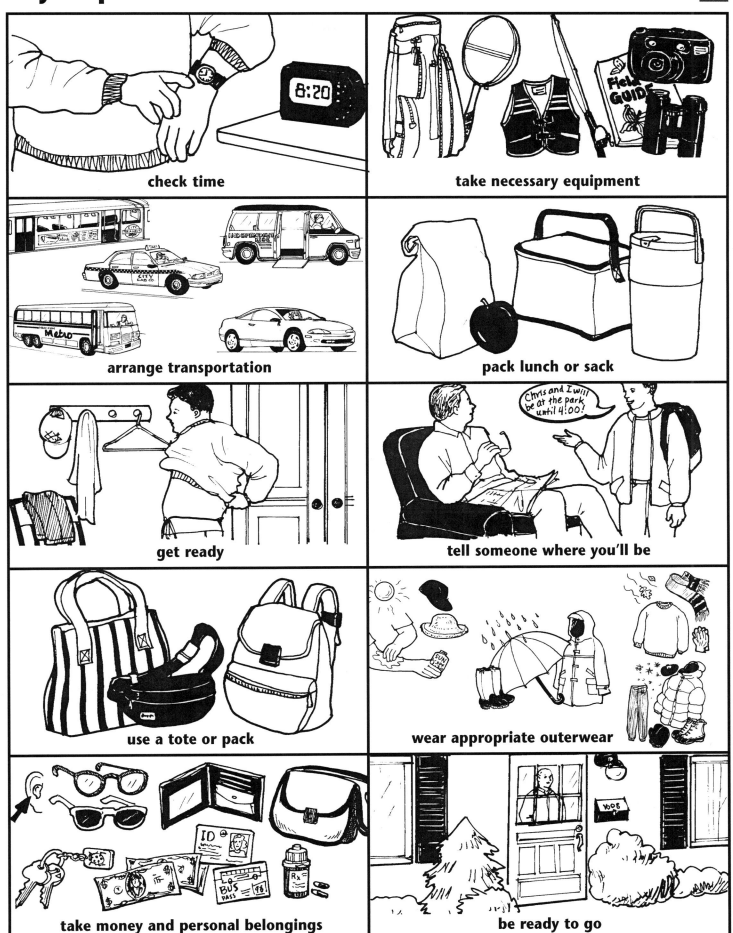

check time

take necessary equipment

arrange transportation

pack lunch or sack

get ready

tell someone where you'll be

use a tote or pack

wear appropriate outerwear

take money and personal belongings

be ready to go

Packing Your Bag

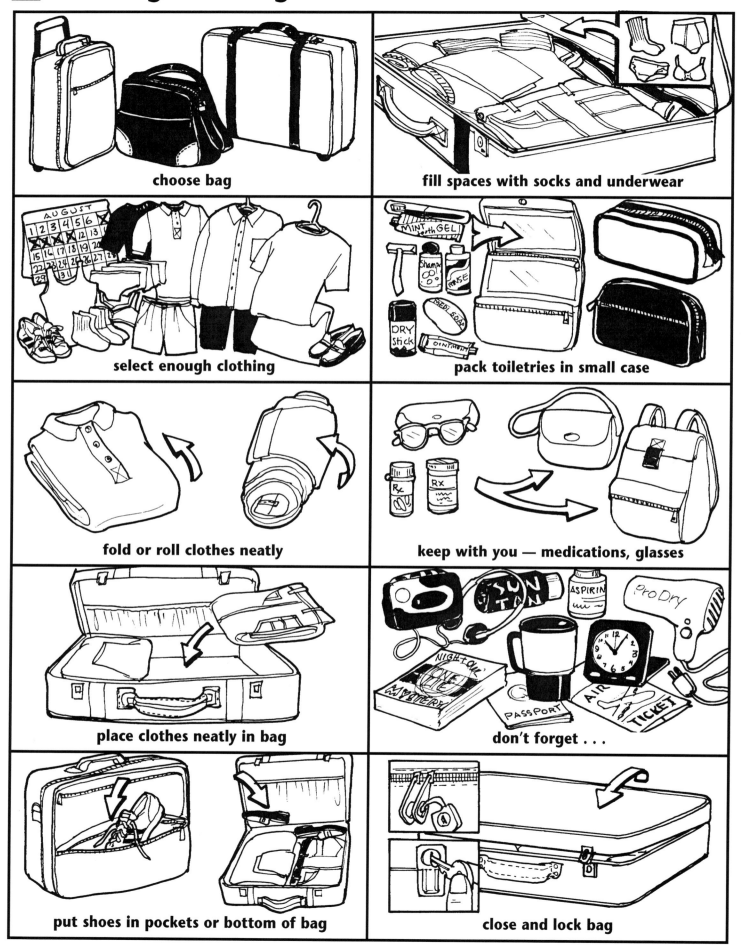

choose bag

fill spaces with socks and underwear

select enough clothing

pack toiletries in small case

fold or roll clothes neatly

keep with you — medications, glasses

place clothes neatly in bag

don't forget . . .

put shoes in pockets or bottom of bag

close and lock bag

Vacation

call for transportation reservations

take money, travelers checks, credit cards

arrange a place to stay

get photo and passport

get tour guide brochures

get necessary vaccinations

pick up and pay for airline tickets

arrange house care

purchase needed items

pack bags

Social Skills: Hotel — Motel

Keep the volume low so you don't disturb others.

The toiletries are for you to use.

The towels and bedding belong to the hotel!

Avoid the "Courtesy Bar" items — they are VERY expensive.

Social Skills: Hotel — Motel

Close the drapes so no one can look in at you.

Call the desk if you need extra towels or soap.

Never open the door unless you are expecting someone.

Be sure you know what time to check out.

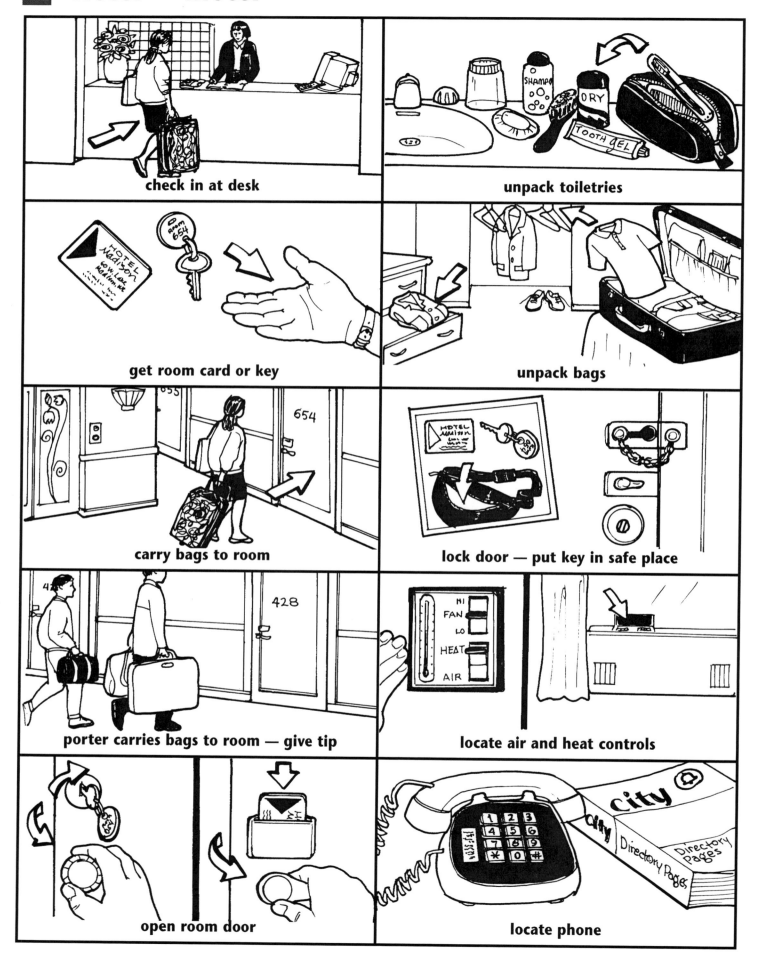

check in at desk

unpack toiletries

get room card or key

unpack bags

carry bags to room

lock door — put key in safe place

porter carries bags to room — give tip

locate air and heat controls

open room door

locate phone

freshen up

wake up call

restaurant   room service

plan your day

pool   health club

pack up everything

ice   vending area

collect belongings — check yourself over

watch TV

check out and pay

choose where to sit

lock your door

open the door

ask before adjusting

sit in the car

unfasten seat belt

close the door/watch for fingers

open the door and get out

fasten your seat belt

close the door — watch for fingers

Gas Station

open gas tank — remove cap

dispense gas — lock pump on

DO YOU WANT A RECEIPT?

use credit card

turn off pump

replace pump handle

SUPER 92   MID-GRADE 89   UNLEADED 87

select type of gas

replace gas cap

close door

insert nozzle in gas tank

10.00
THIS SALE $
7.942
GALLONS
1.259
PRICE PER GALLON

note pump total

turn on pump

pay cashier—use restroom—make other purchases

Social Skills: Bus

Offer your seat to those who need it more.

Give space to others.

You may have to stand if all the seats are taken.

Use your headphones in case others prefer quiet.

Social Skills: Bus

It's OK to ask the driver for help or directions.

Tell the driver if there's a problem.

Ignore rude or loud people.

On a trip, close and lock the bathroom door.

know which route

tell driver your destination — ask for transfer

have correct change, pass or token

find an empty seat

locate bus stop

ride quietly — protect belongings

wait for passengers to exit

signal your stop

get on bus — pay — show pass

exit bus with belongings

Bicycle

wear . . . safety gear and bright clothing

ride to the right

learn good biking skills

keep equipment in good shape

obey traffic laws and signs

don't ride on sidewalks — do ride single file

use hand signals

avoid riding at night and in bad weather

be aware of traffic

plan your route

Social Skills: Taxi (Cab)

Give the driver directions if you know them.

It's OK to ride without talking.

Avoid smoking or eating.

Call the taxi company if you leave something in the cab.

Taxi (Cab)

know destination

fasten seat belt

call taxi company for cost and give address

give destination

wait for taxi

when there, pay fee and tip

flag (hail) taxi

exit with belongings

sit in backseat

tip finder

Bill	Tip	Bill	Tip	Bill	Tip	Bill	Tip	Bill	Tip
1.00	.25	6.00	1.00	11.00	1.75	16.00	2.50	21.00	3.25
1.50	.25	6.50	1.00	11.50	1.75	16.50	2.50	21.50	3.25
2.00	.50	7.00	1.00	12.00	2.00	17.00	2.75	22.00	3.50
2.50	.50	7.50	1.25	12.50	2.00	17.50	2.75	22.50	3.50
3.00	.50	8.00	1.25	13.00	2.00	18.00	2.75	23.00	3.50
3.50	.50	8.50	1.25	13.50	2.00	18.50	2.75	23.50	3.50
4.00	.75	9.00	1.50	14.00	2.25	19.00	3.00	24.00	3.75
4.50	.75	9.50	1.50	14.50	2.25	19.50	3.00	24.50	3.75
5.00	.75	10.00	1.50	15.00	2.25	20.00	3.00	25.00	3.75
5.50	.75	10.50	1.50	15.50	2.50	20.50	3.25	25.50	4.00

Social Skills: Airplane

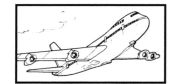

Ask for directions if you can't find your way.

Watch for electric carts in terminals.

It's OK to ask for help or assistance.

Don't carry too much onto the plane.

Social Skills: Airplane

Ask for help if you become ill.

Put your seat upright during meals.

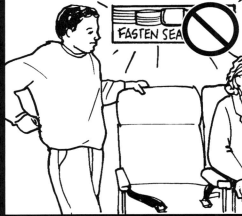

Follow all directions.

Say "excuse me" when moving around others.

gather luggage and ticket

select bags to check

locate check-in for baggage

request seat assignment

locate airline counter

put ticket and boarding pass in safe place

wait in line

find departure gate

present ticket and I.D.

place bags on conveyer

Airplane

walk through detector and pick up your bag

find your assigned seat

proceed to gate

stow bags

wait until your flight is called

fasten your safety belt

get in boarding line

locate light and air controls

show boarding pass to attendant

ask for help if needed

occupy your time

collect belongings

food and beverage is served

exit as aisle clears

find bathroom(s)

exit plane

prepare for landing

collect your baggage

stay seated until notified

exit airline terminal

Social Skills: Commuter Train

Give space to others — don't crowd.

Ignore rude or weird people.

If you are too slow, the doors will close.

To be safe, go with a friend when you ride at night.

know which line

deposit fare and go through turnstile

enter departure station

find waiting area

locate your ticket counter

ask for help

buy tokens or fare card

stand safely away from track

buy tokens or ticket

identify correct train

wait for passengers to exit

don't stare

avoid empty cars

hold onto bar

find an empty seat

identify correct stop

protect your belongings

exit with belongings

give ticket to conductor

exit station and determine your location

Shopping

Activity List

Social Skills: Grocery Store
Grocery Store
Grocery Unpacking
Social Skills: Department Store
Department Store
Department Store Returns
Department Store Locations
Social Skills: Clothing Purchase
Clothing Purchase
Your New Clothes
Pharmacy
Social Skills: Vending Machine
Vending Machine

Social Skills: Grocery Store

Push your cart carefully so you don't bump into displays or shoppers.

Handle with care so you don't drop or damage anything.

When your cart blocks the aisle, no one can get by.

If you leave your belongings in your cart, someone may steal them.

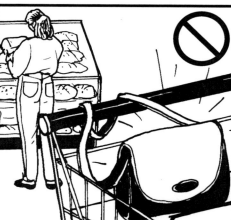

Social Skills: Grocery Store

It's not yours to eat until you pay for it.

Cutting in line is rude.

Choose the right lane for the items you're buying.

Stealing is against the law!

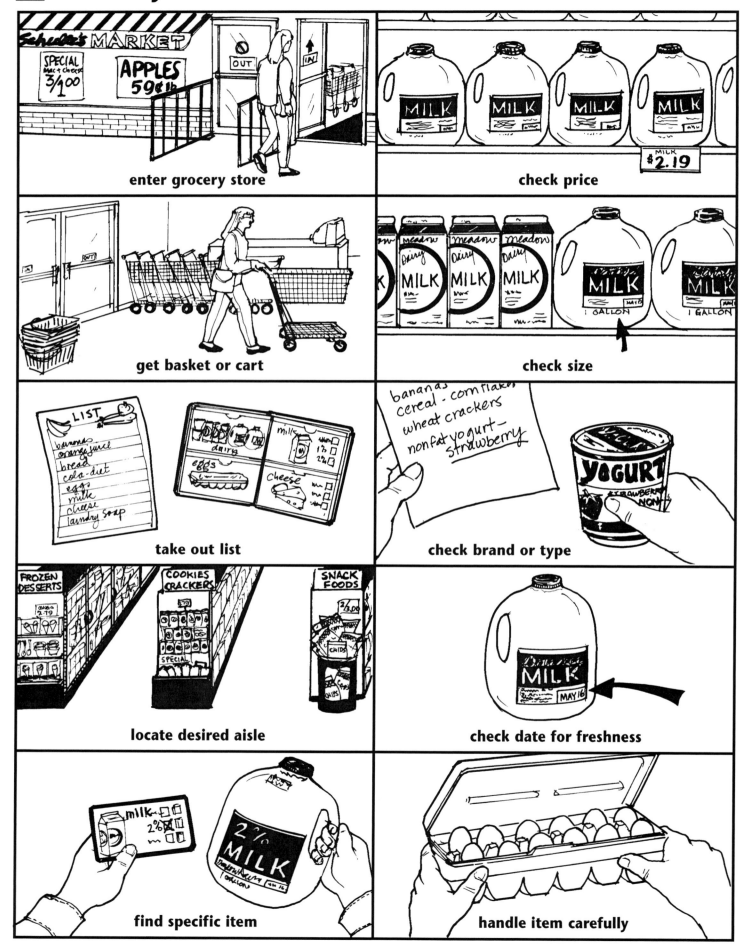

enter grocery store

check price

get basket or cart

check size

take out list

check brand or type

locate desired aisle

check date for freshness

find specific item

handle item carefully

Grocery Store

arrange items in cart

go ahead as line moves

go on to next item

get money ready

select checkout lane

put items on counter

use express lane

greet cashier and give coupons

go to the end of the line

choose paper or plastic bags

Grocery Store

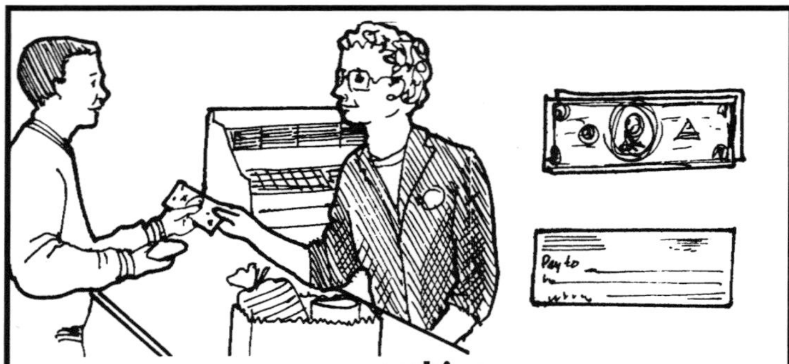

pay cashier

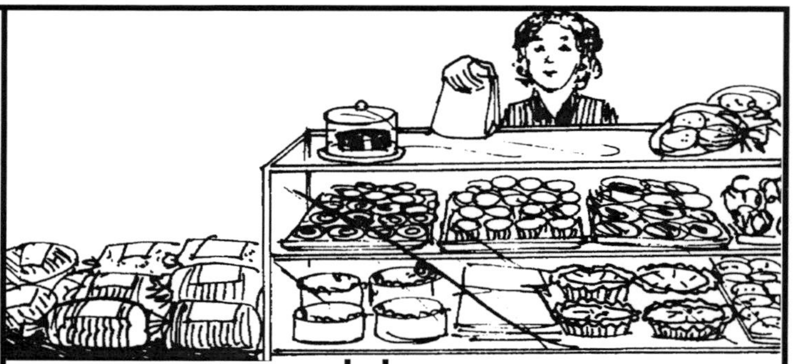

bakery

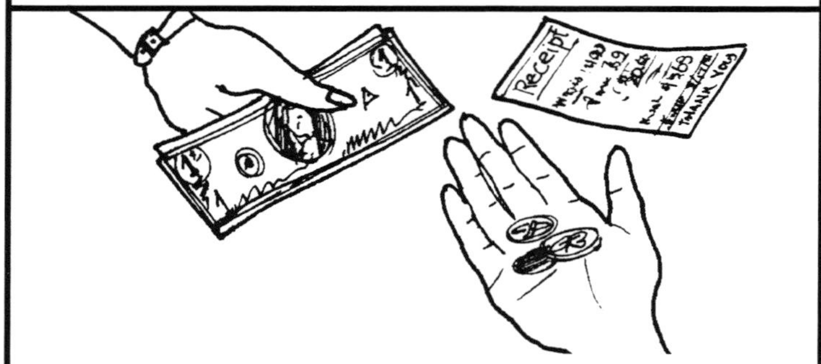

get change

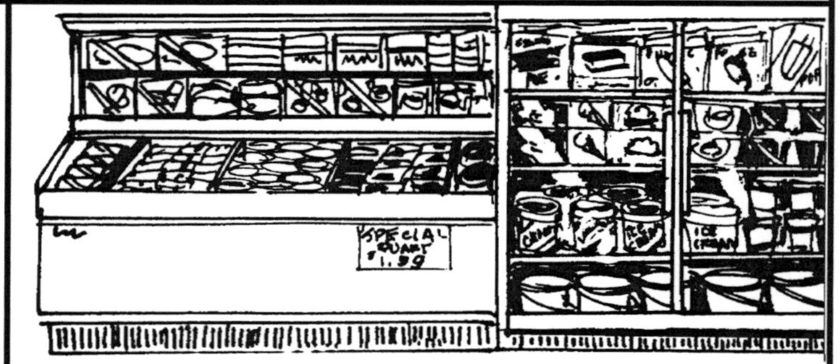

frozen foods

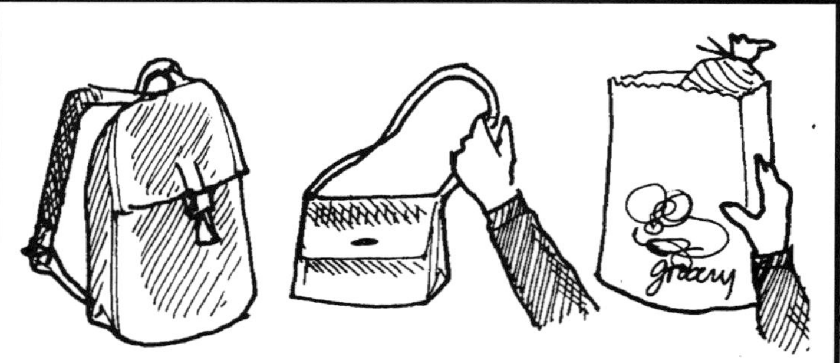

take bags and belongings

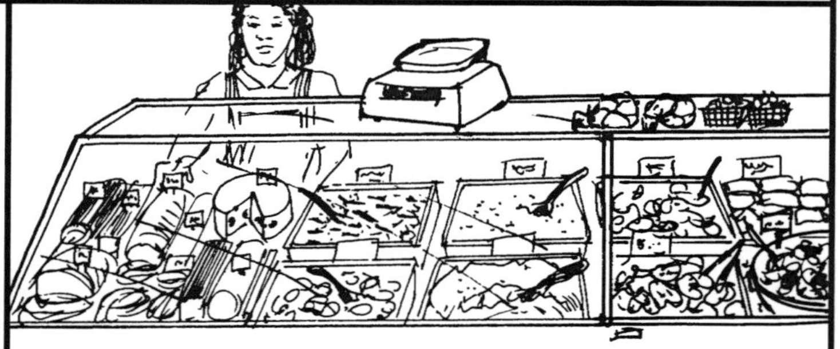

deli

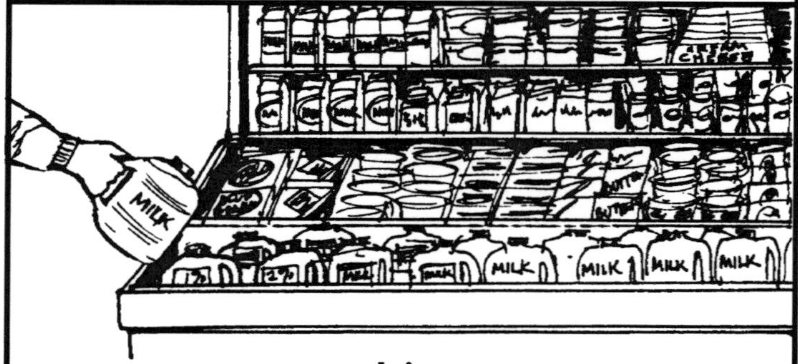

dairy

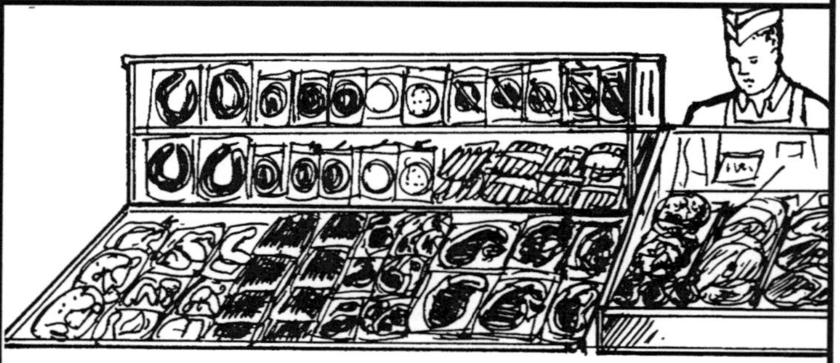

meat

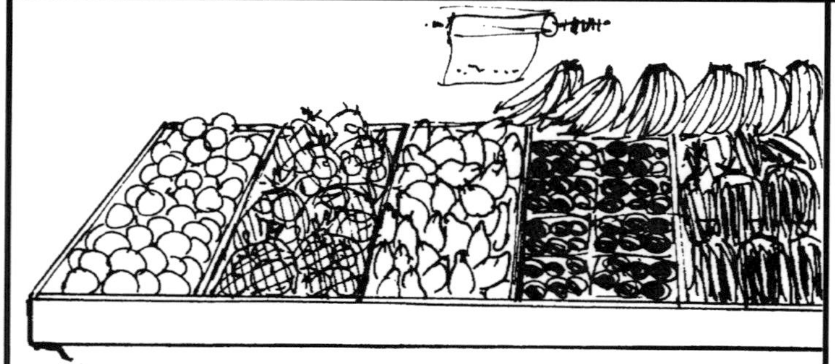

produce

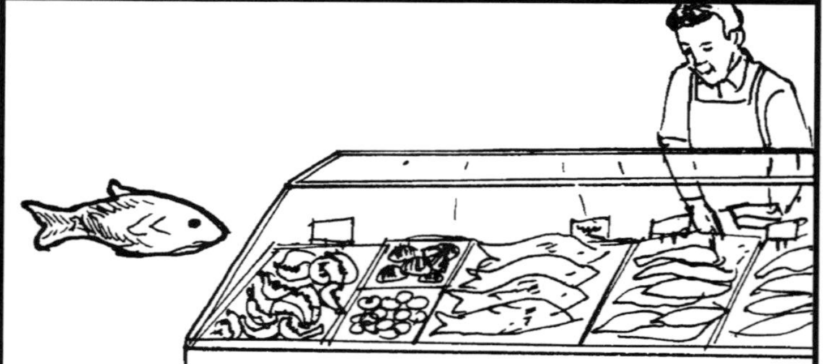

fish

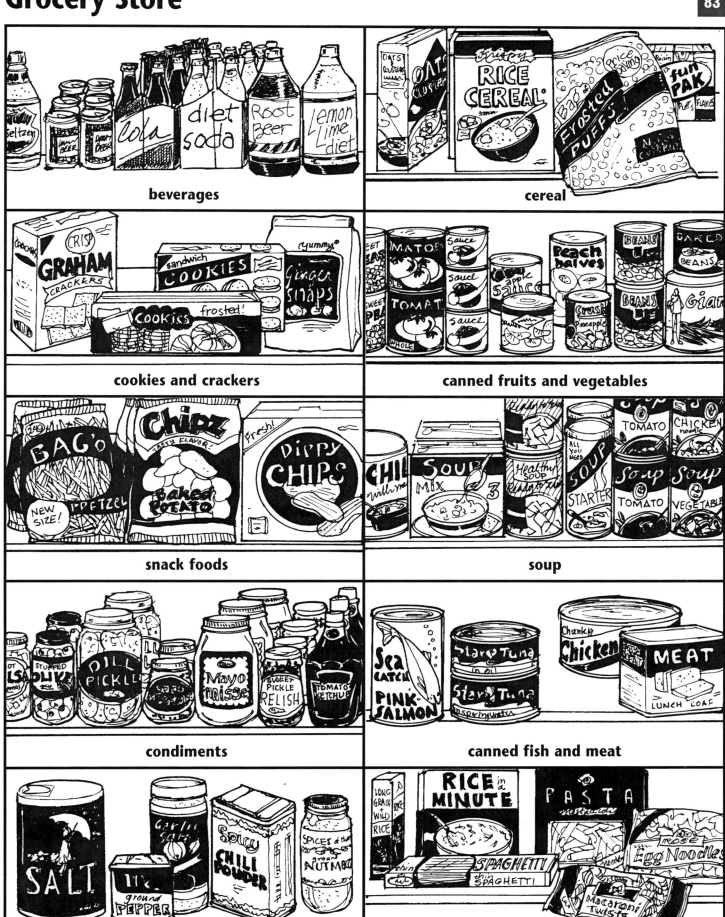

beverages

cereal

cookies and crackers

canned fruits and vegetables

snack foods

soup

condiments

canned fish and meat

spices and herbs

rice and pasta

bread

ethnic foods

coffee and tea

health and diet foods

liquor

baby products

candy

pet needs

baking supplies

paper products

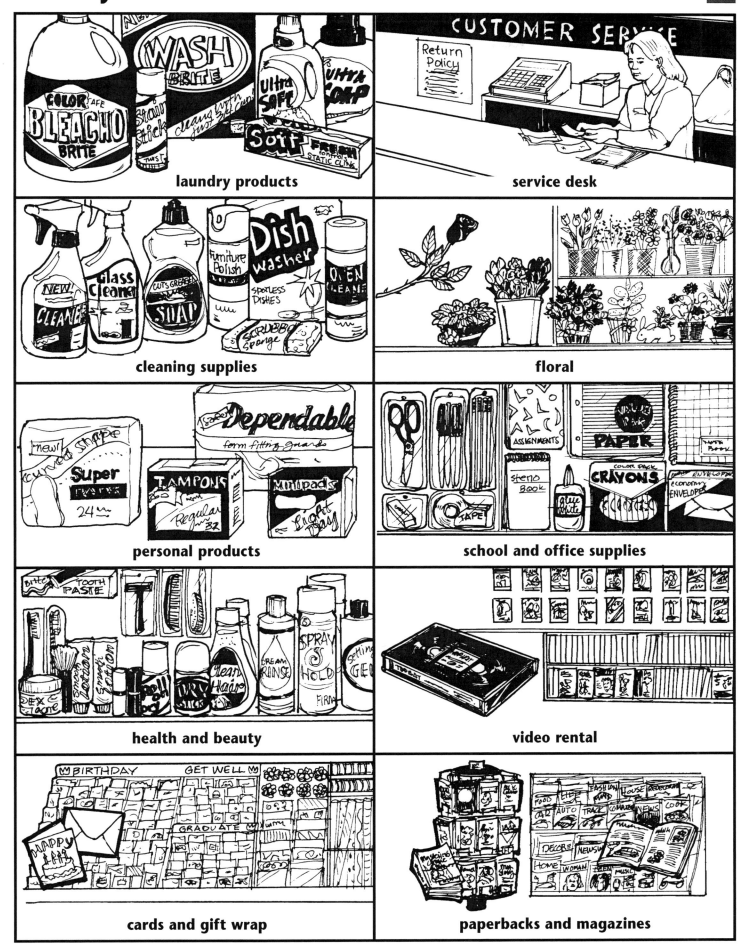

laundry products

service desk

cleaning supplies

floral

personal products

school and office supplies

health and beauty

video rental

cards and gift wrap

paperbacks and magazines

Grocery Unpacking

86

put bags on counter

put items under sink

empty bags

put other items away

put freezer items away

discard unneeded packaging

put refrigerated items away

put grocery bags away

put cupboard items away

refile shopping cards

Social Skills: Department Store

Handle merchandise only if you think you'll buy.

Ask for help if you can't reach or find something.

If you need an item from a display case, ask a clerk for help.

Put things back neatly after you've looked at them.

Social Skills: Department Store

If you're polite, you'll get better service.

Wait patiently for your turn.

Push your cart carefully so you don't bump into people or merchandise.

Stealing is against the law!

Department Store

enter store

locate checkout area

get cart or basket

get money ready

decide where to go

pay for purchase

handle items carefully

get change and receipt

ask for help

collect belongings

Department Store Returns

locate service desk

clothing

present item and receipts

baby

give information

shoes

receive refund

toys

exit store

pets

Department Store Locations

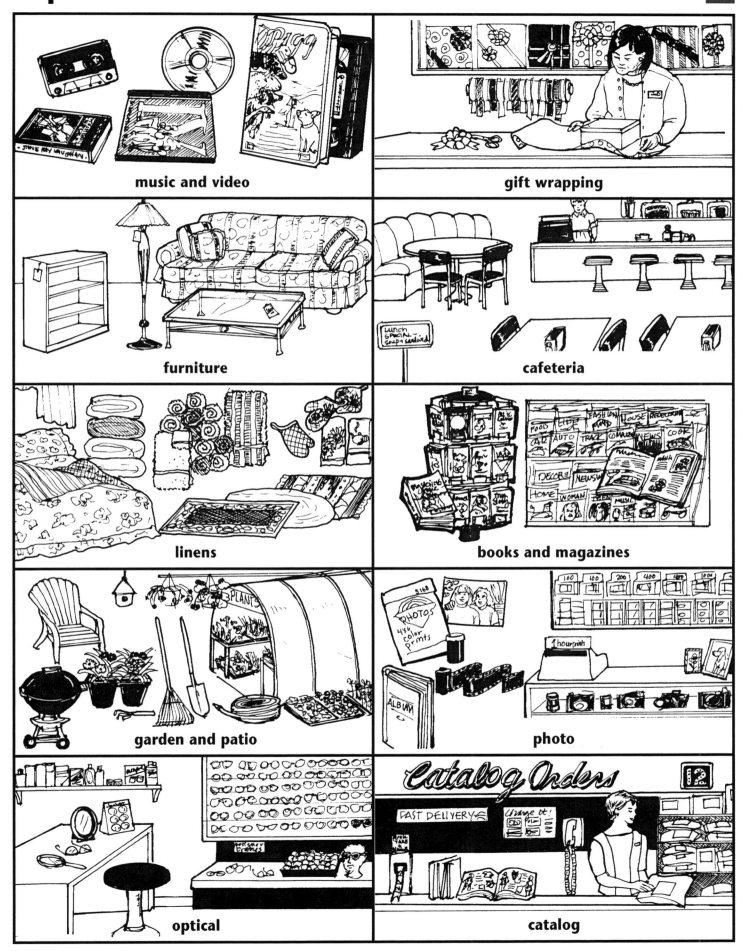

music and video

gift wrapping

furniture

cafeteria

linens

books and magazines

garden and patio

photo

optical

catalog

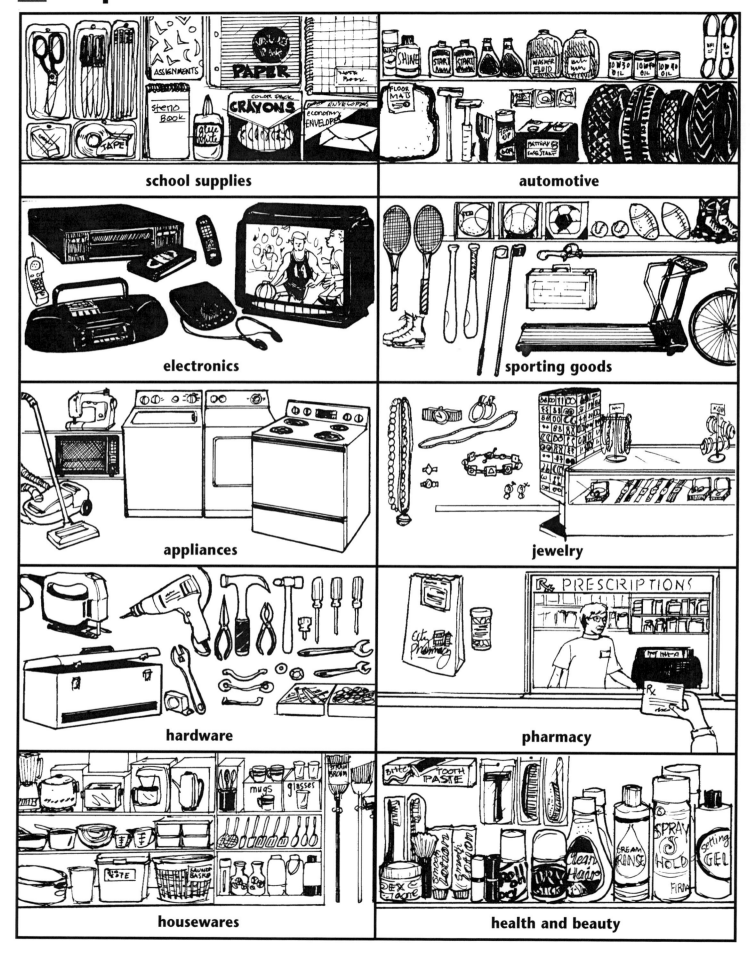

school supplies

automotive

electronics

sporting goods

appliances

jewelry

hardware

pharmacy

housewares

health and beauty

Social Skills: Clothing Purchase

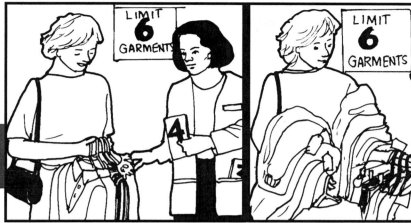

Know how many items you can try on at a time.

The fitting room should be empty. Knock first.

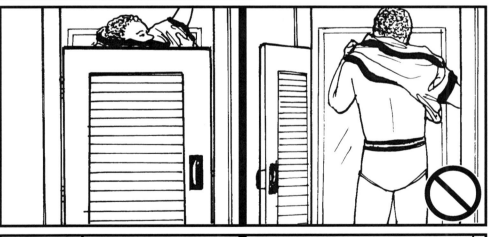

Close your door when you try on clothes.

Don't leave a mess in the fitting room!

boys' department

choose clothes

girls' department

ask for help

men's wear

locate fitting rooms

women's wear

get item number from clerk

athletic wear

choose vacant fitting room

Clothing Purchase

lock fitting room door

leave fitting room

hang up clothes

return unwanted clothes

try on clothes

find cashier

check yourself over

ready money, check or credit card

get dressed

pay and save receipt

Your New Clothes

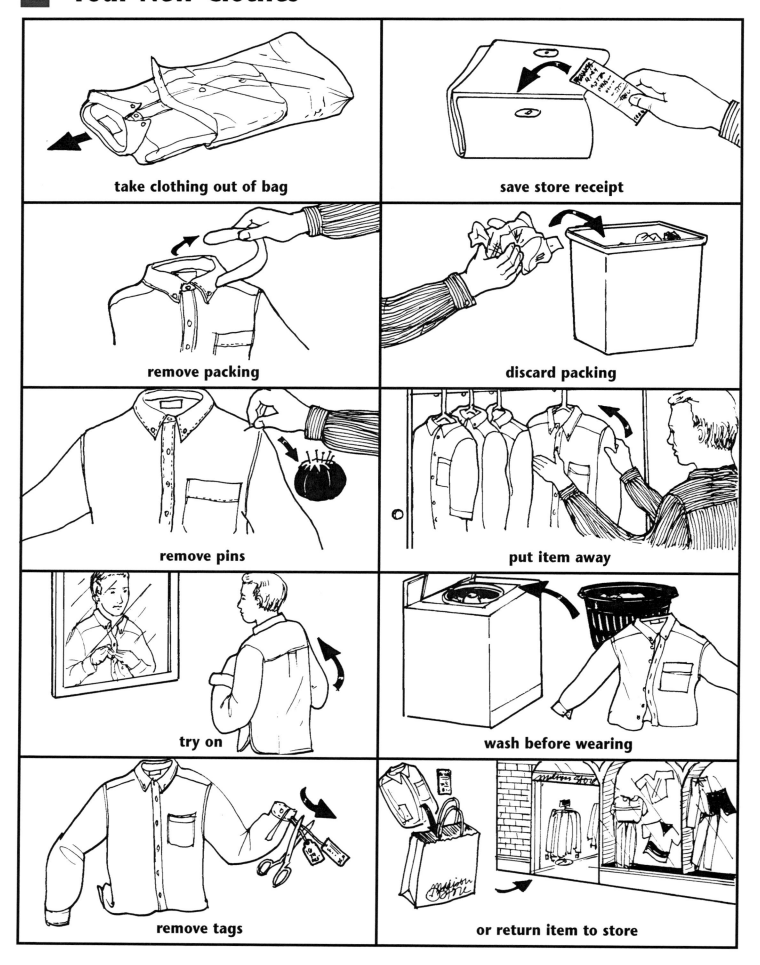

take clothing out of bag

save store receipt

remove packing

discard packing

remove pins

put item away

try on

wash before wearing

remove tags

or return item to store

Pharmacy

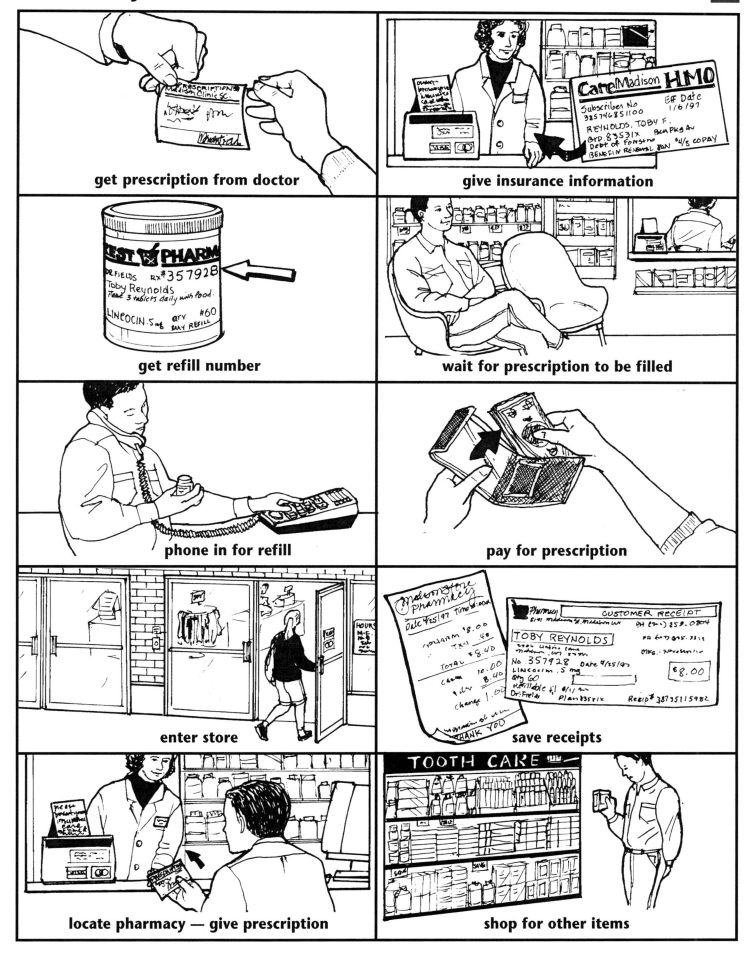

get prescription from doctor

give insurance information

get refill number

wait for prescription to be filled

phone in for refill

pay for prescription

enter store

save receipts

locate pharmacy — give prescription

shop for other items

Social Skills: Vending Machine

Wait patiently for your turn.

Shaking the machine is dangerous.

Eat and drink only where allowed.

Dispose of waste properly.

Vending Machine

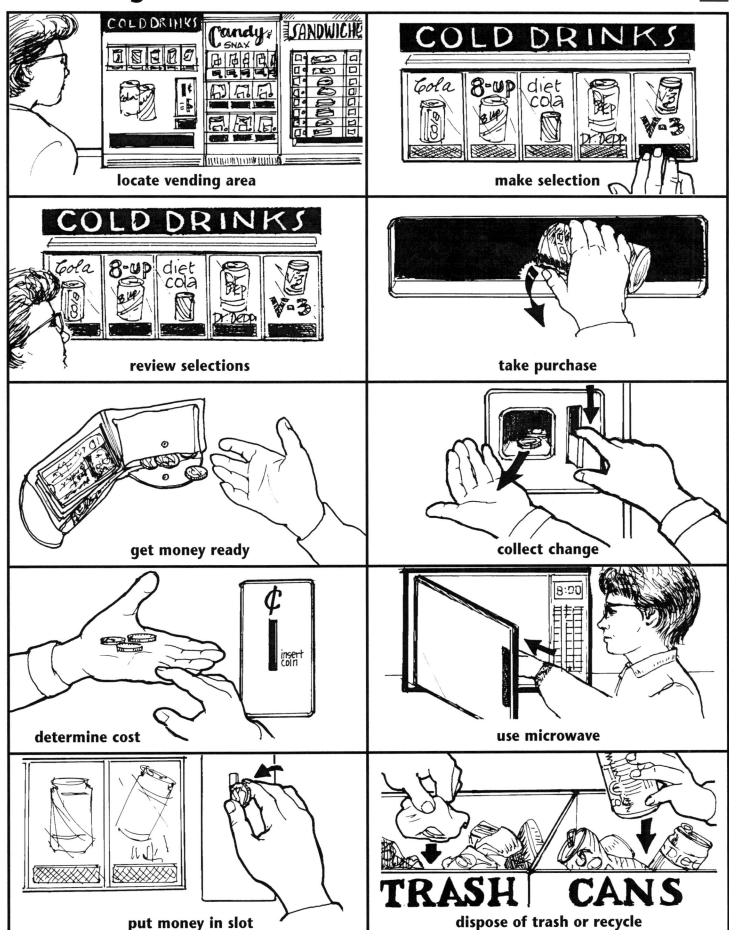

locate vending area

make selection

review selections

take purchase

get money ready

collect change

determine cost

use microwave

put money in slot

dispose of trash or recycle

Eating Out

Community SUCCESS

Activity List

Table Manners
General Dining
Social Skills: Fast Food
Fast Food
Social Skills: Fast Food—Drive Thru
Fast Food—Drive Thru
Ordering a Pizza
Social Skills: Table Service
Table Service
Social Skills: Buffet
Buffet
Social Skills: Cafeteria
Cafeteria
Social Skills: Dinner Invitation
Dinner Invitation

Table Manners

Table Manners

put napkin on lap ➡ not OK

use your napkin ➡ not OK

use utensils ➡ not OK

Please pass the salt!

pass condiments ➡ not OK

use condiments ➡ not OK

Table Manners

I have reservations.

I would like to sit at a . . . .

booth | table | window seat

Do you accept checks?

Do you accept credit cards?

One bill is fine.

Separate checks, please.

non-smoking | smoking section

Could you carry this for me, please?

May I have the bill, please?

Where do I pay?

General Dining

WOMEN MEN restroom | coat rack | pay phone

dietary restrictions

Where is the . . . .

This is not my order.

Please wrap this.

Everything is fine, thank you.

Please bring more. . . .

 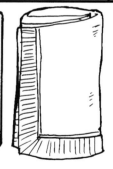   

I would like . . . .

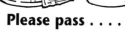

Please pass . . . .

Social Skills: **Fast Food**

Know what you want before you go to the counter.

Wash your hands before eating.

Remember your table manners.

Don't take others' food unless they share it.

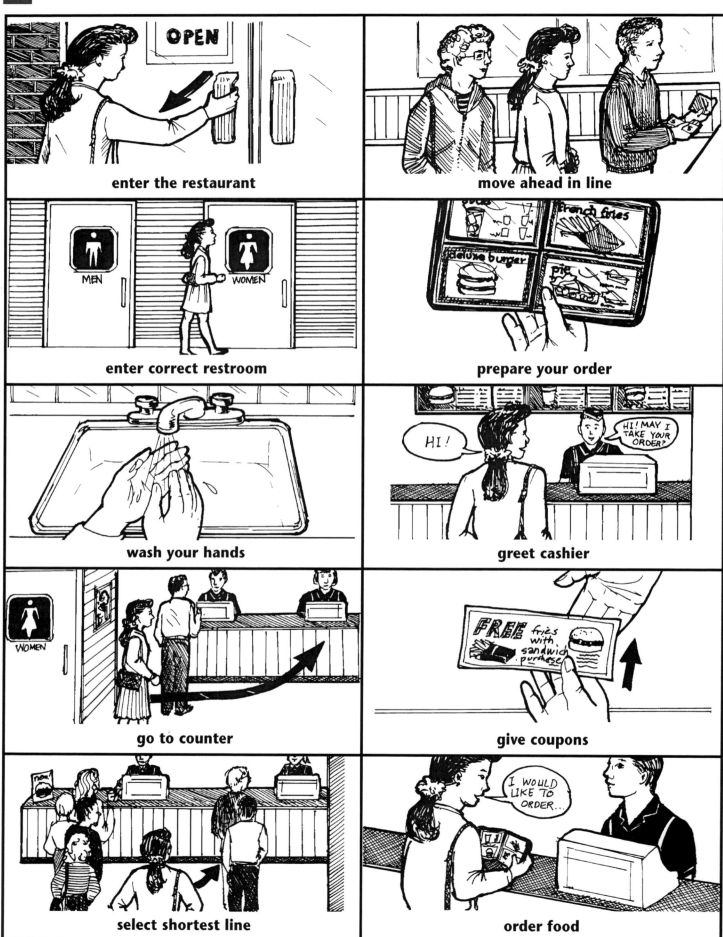

enter the restaurant

move ahead in line

enter correct restroom

prepare your order

wash your hands

greet cashier

go to counter

give coupons

select shortest line

order food

Fast Food

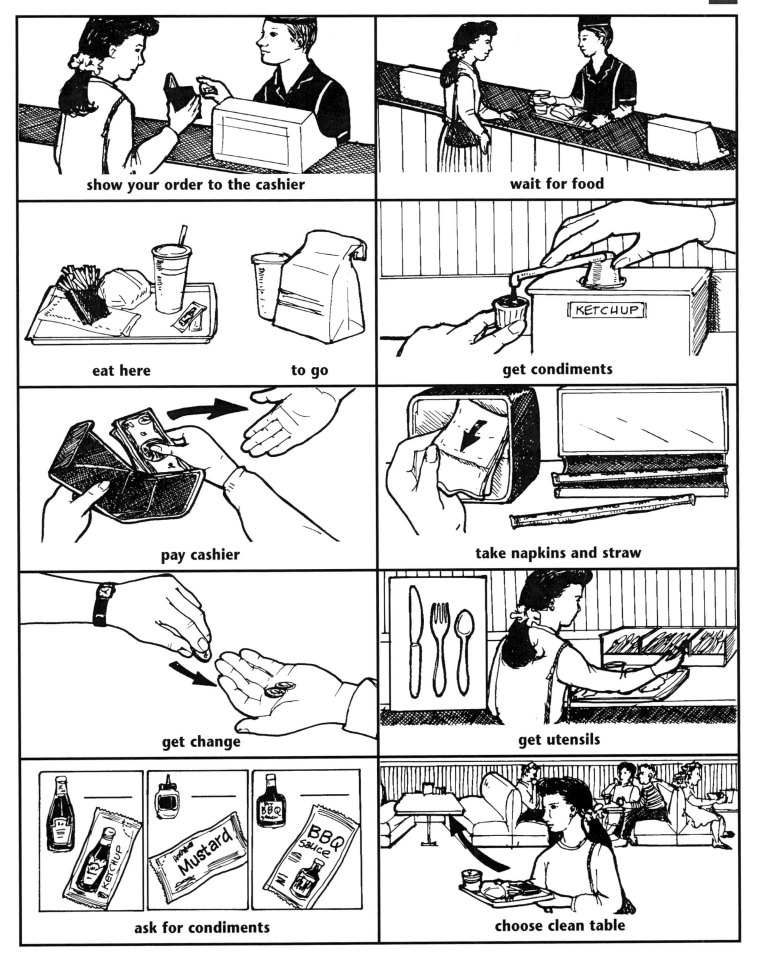

show your order to the cashier

wait for food

eat here

to go

get condiments

pay cashier

take napkins and straw

get change

get utensils

ask for condiments

choose clean table

Fast Food

carry tray carefully

collect belongings

put tray on table

carry tray to counter

eat neatly

put trash in container

talk nicely

stack tray

clean table

exit restaurant

Social Skills: Fast Food — Drive Thru

Know what you want before you drive up.

Once you've ordered, don't change your mind.

Speak loudly and clearly into the microphone.

Check your order before you drive away.

choose type of food

speak order clearly

decide where to go

mention coupons

look at menu board

listen to order and cost

check coupons

correct order if necessary

decide what to order

prepare money and coupons

Fast Food — Drive Thru

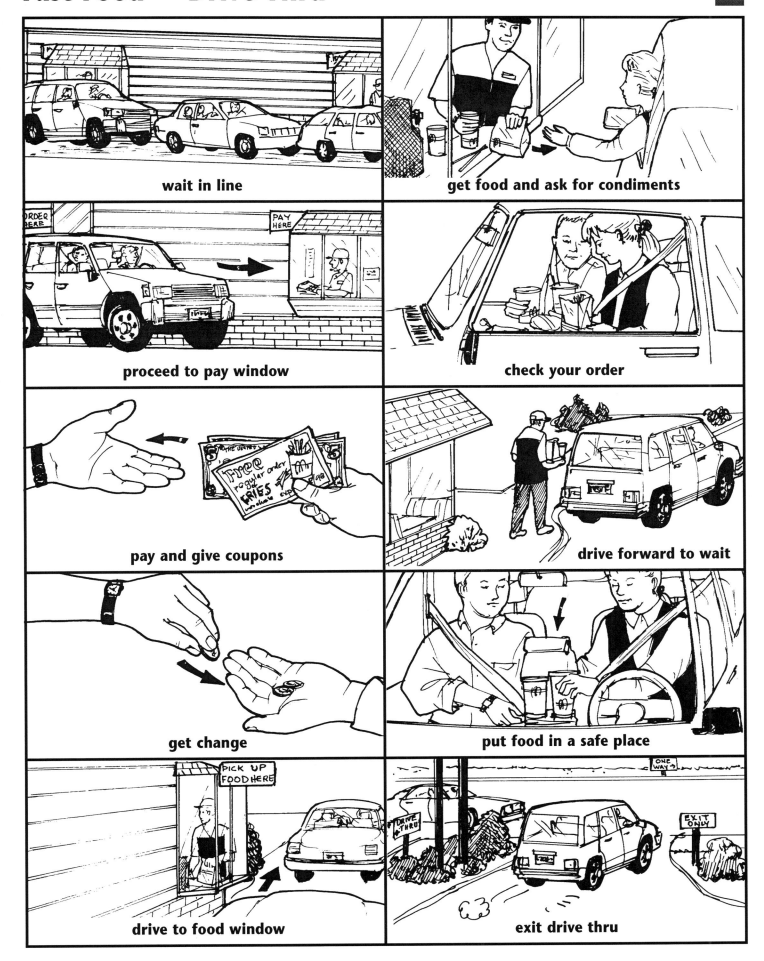

wait in line

get food and ask for condiments

proceed to pay window

check your order

pay and give coupons

drive forward to wait

get change

put food in a safe place

drive to food window

exit drive thru

Ordering a Pizza

decide what to eat

look up phone number

size

dial number

toppings

give order clearly

I'D LIKE TO ORDER A PIZZA ...

type

ADDRESS

PHONE

give address and phone

review coupons

TIME

COST

delivery time and cost

Ordering a Pizza

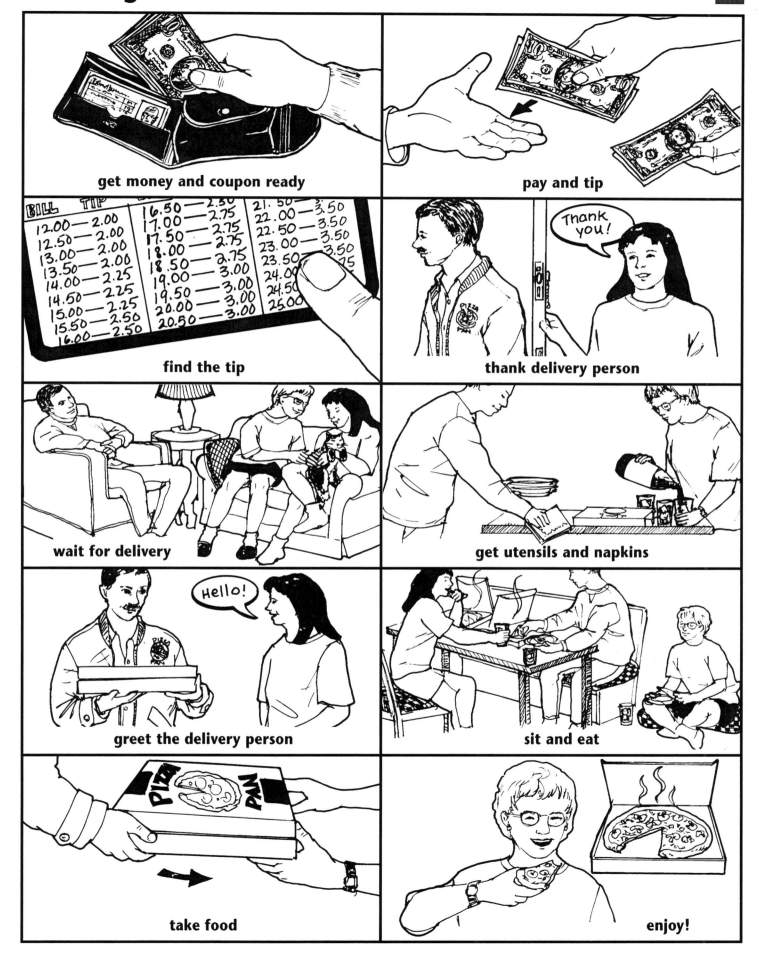

get money and coupon ready

pay and tip

find the tip

thank delivery person

wait for delivery

get utensils and napkins

greet the delivery person

sit and eat

take food

enjoy!

Social Skills: Table Service

Be on time if you have a reservation.

Know the dress code.

Wash your hands before you eat.

Remember your table manners!

Table Service

enter restaurant

a table for _____, please

check coat   **hang coat**

table   **booth**   **counter**

Hello! Two for dinner, please!

greet host

follow host to table

Please wait to be seated

wait to be seated

say thank you!

no smoking, please

look at menu

greet server

go to salad bar

ask for separate bills

take condiments or crackers

order beverage

thank server

order food

use correct restroom

wait patiently

order dessert

Table Service

eat neatly

pay server

wait for change

talk nicely

pay cashier

wait for change

ask for service

collect belongings

review bill

get coat

leave tip

exit restaurant

Social Skills: Buffet

Go to the end of the line — don't cut in.

Use utensils to take food.

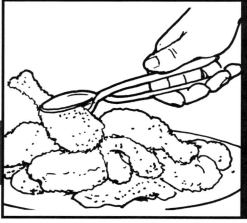

Never put food back after you've touched it.

Take a clean plate if you go back for more.

Buffet

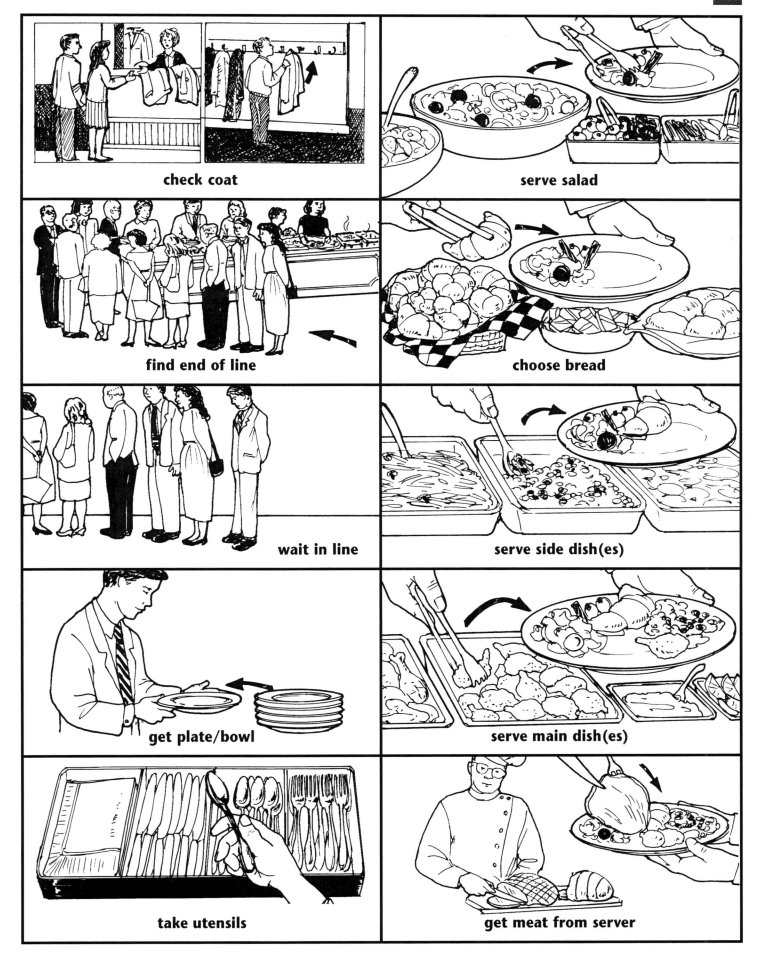

check coat

serve salad

find end of line

choose bread

wait in line

serve side dish(es)

get plate/bowl

serve main dish(es)

take utensils

get meat from server

take dessert

give beverage order to server

I'd like a please!

select beverage

eat neatly

get condiments

talk nicely

carry food to table

return for more

arrange dishes and utensils

take clean plate

Buffet

choose seconds or dessert

collect belongings

get bill and review

pay cashier and get change

get money ready

thank you very much

leave tip

get coat

pay server and get change

exit buffet

Social Skills: Cafeteria

It's rude to cut in line.

Don't put food back.

Buy only what you can eat.

Make your choices promptly.

Cafeteria

enter restaurant

select side dish

go to counter

choose main dish

take a tray

select dessert

get utensils

take beverage

choose salad

get money ready

Cafeteria

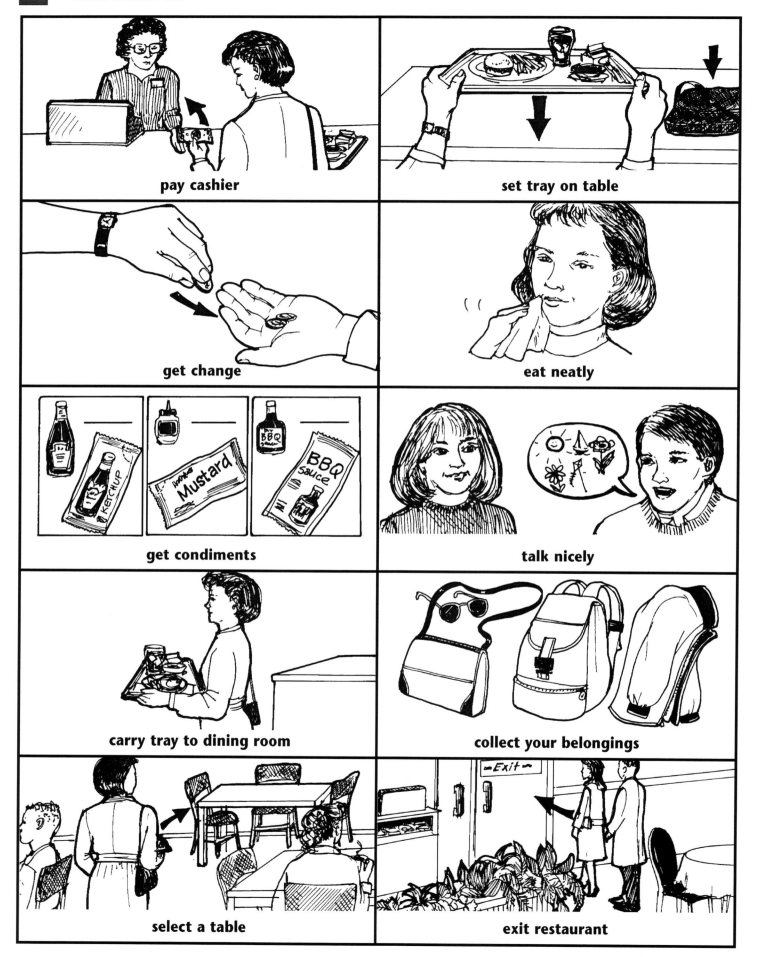

pay cashier

set tray on table

get change

eat neatly

get condiments

talk nicely

carry tray to dining room

collect your belongings

select a table

exit restaurant

Social Skills: Dinner Invitation

If you're early, they won't be ready. If you're late, they'll be upset.

A hostess gift is a good idea.

Be a polite eater.

If you stay too late, you may not be invited again.

Dinner Invitation

Community SUCCESS

Appointment Please

Activity List

Social Skills: Telephone
Telephone Appointment
Social Skills: Waiting Room
Waiting Room
Social Skills: Clinic
Doctor
Medical Procedures
Medical Specialties
Social Skills: Dentist
Dentist
Optometrist — Eye Exam
Optometrist — Glasses
Social Skills: Veterinarian
Veterinarian
Social Skills: Hair Salon and Barber
Hair Salon
Barber

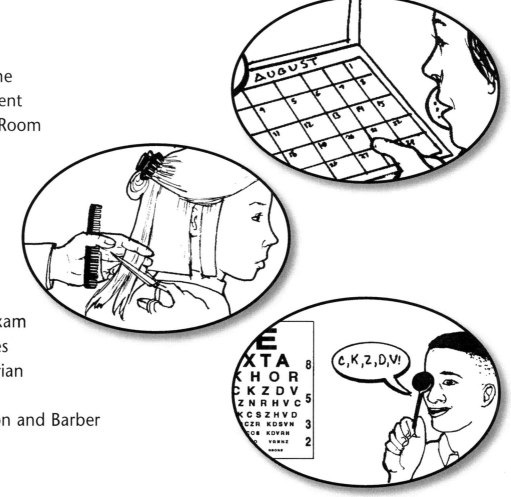

Social Skills: **Telephone**

Speak clearly so you can be heard.

Don't answer personal questions or buy things from strangers.

Making crank calls is illegal!

Don't call very early or late at night.

Telephone Appointment

find phone number

ask for a specific time/date

dial phone number

confirm time and date

request appointment

write time and date on calendar

reason for appointment

thank you

give necessary information

hang up telephone

Social Skills: Waiting Room

Be on time for your appointment or it may be cancelled.

Call if you are going to be late.

Bring something to occupy your time.

Let the receptionist know if you use the restroom.

Waiting Room

enter waiting area

wait quietly   wait patiently

go to reception desk

protect your belongings

give your name and appointment time

occupy your time

hang up your coat

follow when your name is called

be seated

please let me know when my name is called

Social Skills: Clinic

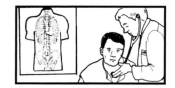

Be sure you are neat and clean.

Make a list of problems or questions to ask.

You can get handouts to answer many questions.

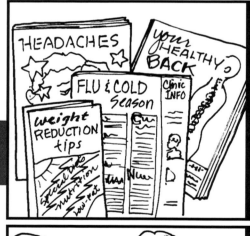

Take friend or relative along to help you understand and communicate.

Doctor

check in/get patient form

temperature

weigh-in

when you are called, follow to exam room

tell all medications you take

be seated

follow undressing directions

give patient form — tell reason for visit

wait on exam table

have blood pressure and pulse taken

greet the doctor

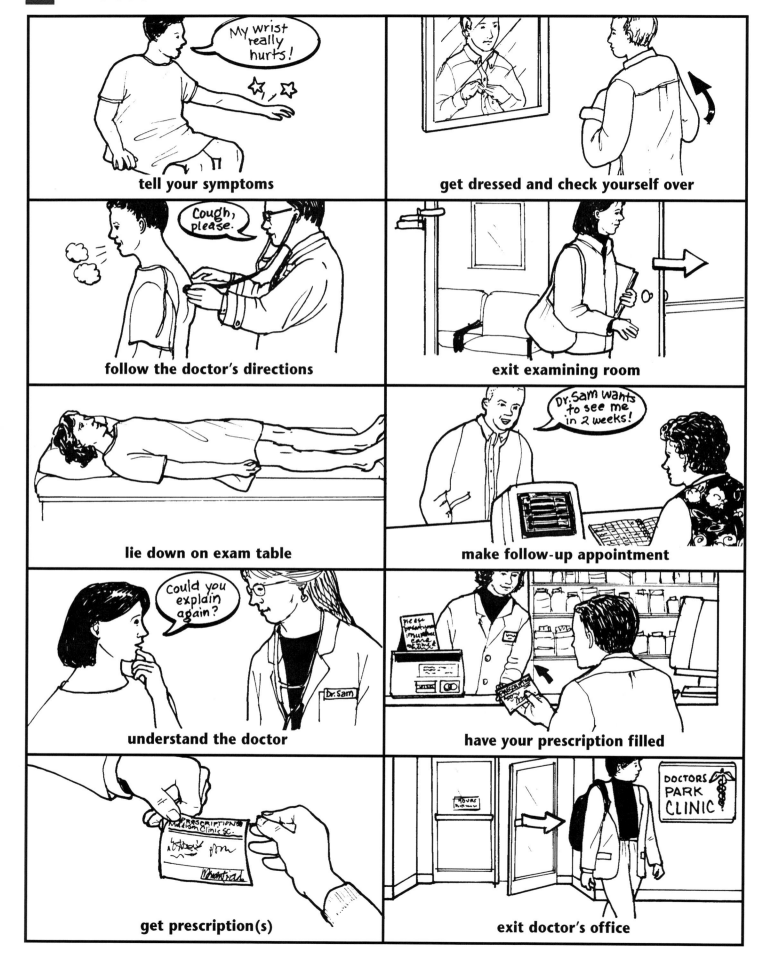

Medical Procedures

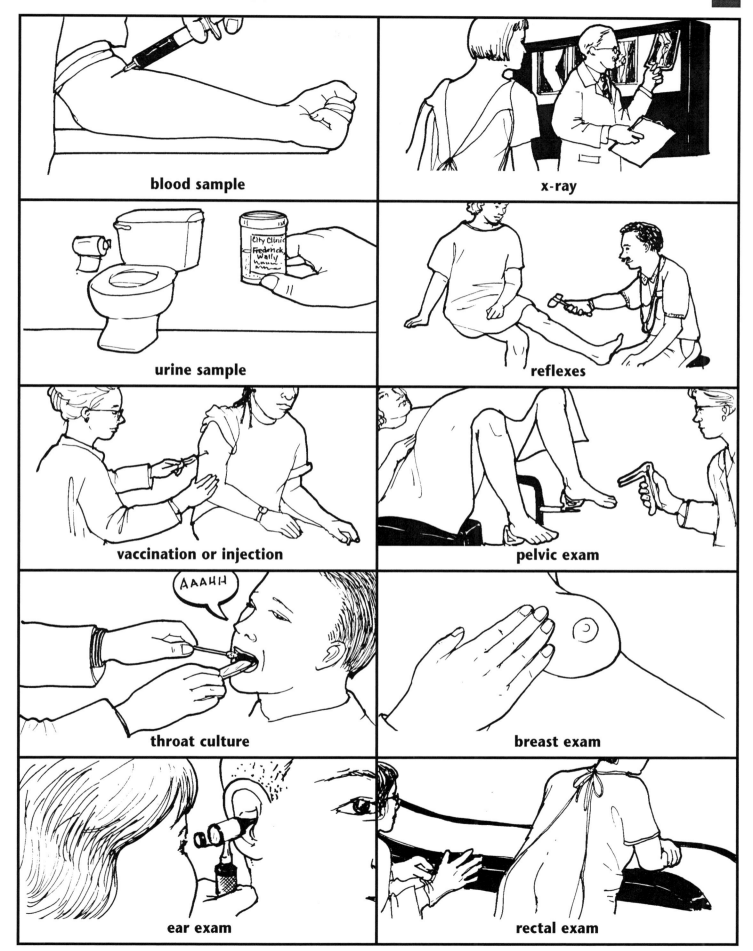

blood sample

x-ray

urine sample

reflexes

vaccination or injection

pelvic exam

throat culture

AAAHH

breast exam

ear exam

rectal exam

Medical Specialties

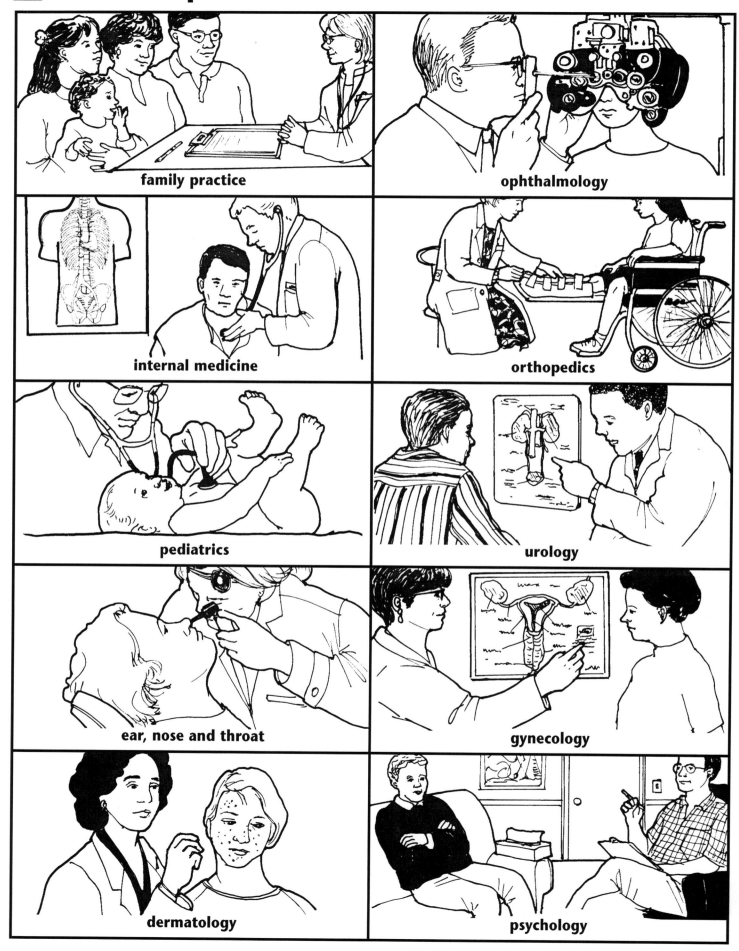

family practice

ophthalmology

internal medicine

orthopedics

pediatrics

urology

ear, nose and throat

gynecology

dermatology

psychology

Social Skills: Dentist

Brush your teeth thoroughly before you go.

Take pre-medication if necessary.

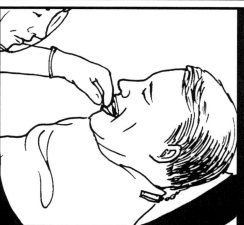

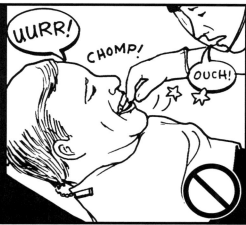

Do not bite or make loud noises.

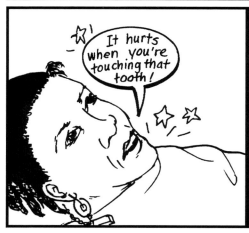

Tell the dentist if you feel pain.

Dentist

check in at reception desk

discuss dental problems and payment plan

sit and wait until called

open mouth — relax

follow to examining room

follow instructions

be seated — chair is adjusted

dental x-rays

wear clothing protector

teeth cleaning

Dentist

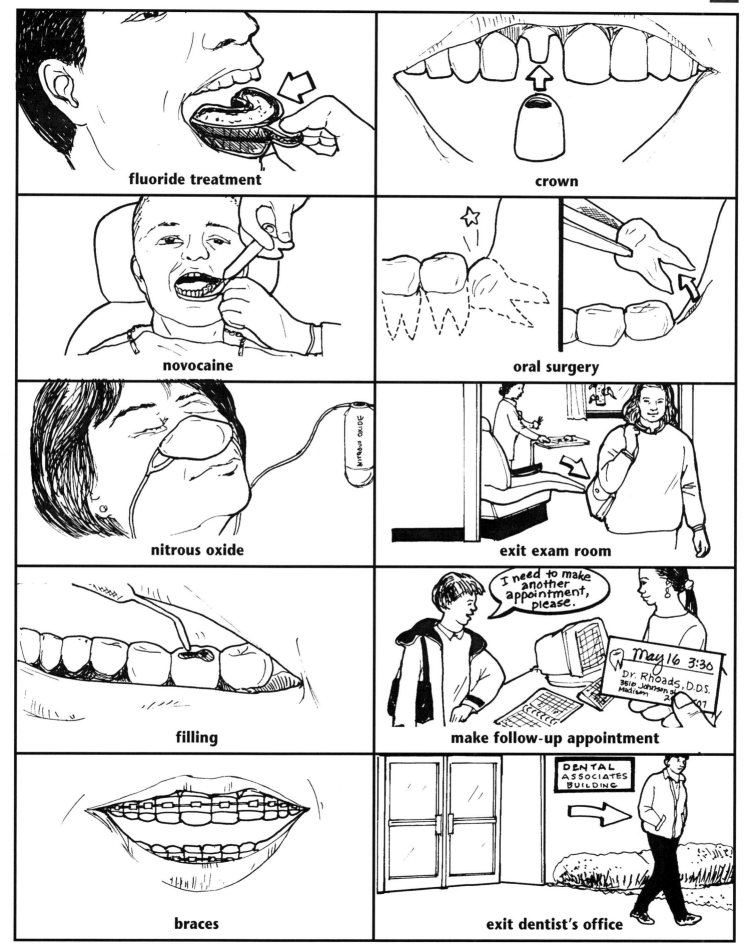

fluoride treatment

crown

novocaine

oral surgery

nitrous oxide

exit exam room

filling

make follow-up appointment

braces

exit dentist's office

Optometrist — Eye Exam

enter office — check in

glaucoma testing

sit and wait until called

eye examination

go to exam room

read chart

answer eye health questions

prescription exam

eye drops

discuss eyewear options

look at frames

ask advice — make final choice

give prescription to optometrist

optometrist fits frames

select frames to try on

pick up glasses

wait for glasses

sit and try on frames

pay for services/glasses

find out cost and delivery date

exit office

Social Skills: Veterinarian

Walk your dog outside before going into the office.

Take your pet in a cage or on a leash — not loose.

Keep leashed pet close to you so it doesn't bother others.

Help hold your pet while the vet examines.

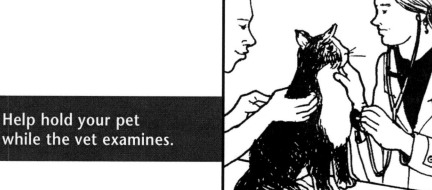
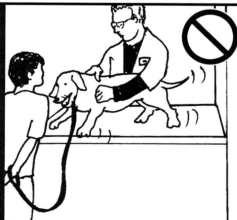

Veterinarian

enter office — check in

listen carefully — make sure you understand

find a quiet place to sit

exit exam room to reception desk

when called, go to exam room

pay bill — get change and receipt

put pet on examining table

get tags and medications — fill out return cards

reason for visit

exit office with pet and belongings

Social Skills: Hair Salon and Barber

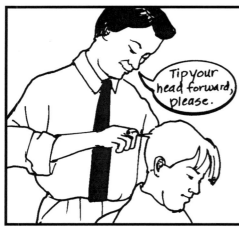

Follow directions.

Be clean and neat. Some places require freshly washed hair, too.

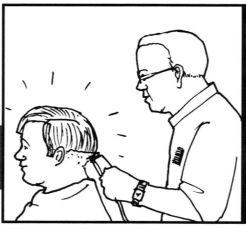

Don't ask for extra services if you haven't scheduled them.

Your hair may not look like the picture!

Hair Salon

enter salon — check in for appointment

discuss procedures and cost

walk in — ask for appointment

show picture of desired style

take a seat until called

shampoo — condition

follow cosmetologist to be seated

haircut

put on cape

trim

Hair Salon

perm

ask how to care for hairstyle at home

relaxing

select haircare products to purchase

styling

blowdry

pay and get change

coloring

give tip

manicure

nails

exit salon with belongings

Barber

enter — check in for appointment

explain how to cut

long
short
over the ears
above the ears
crew cut

enter — walk in for appointment

Can you fit me in for a haircut?

follow directions

Look down, please.

take a seat until called

You're next, Dan!

check/approve cut

I like it!

sit in barber chair

pay and tip

explain what you want

I'd like a haircut, please.

exit with belongings

OPEN
HAIR CUTS

Money Matters

Activity List

Social Skills: Money

Bank

Cash

Check

Credit Card

Social Skills: Automatic Teller Machine (ATM)

Automatic Teller Machine (ATM)

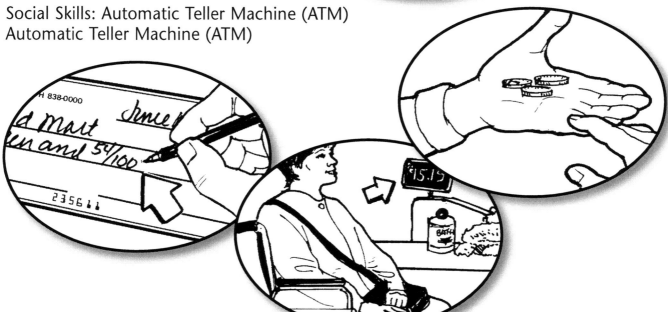

Social Skills: **Money**

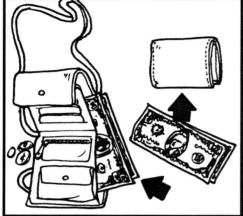

Keep your money safe in a wallet or purse.

Avoid showing how much money you have.

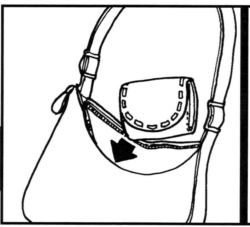

Avoid talking about how much money you have.

It's not a good idea to loan your money — you may not get it back.

Bank

enter bank

give materials to teller

go to counter or table

wait for transaction

get forms

get receipt or cash

complete forms

count and put away money items

wait in line for teller

exit bank

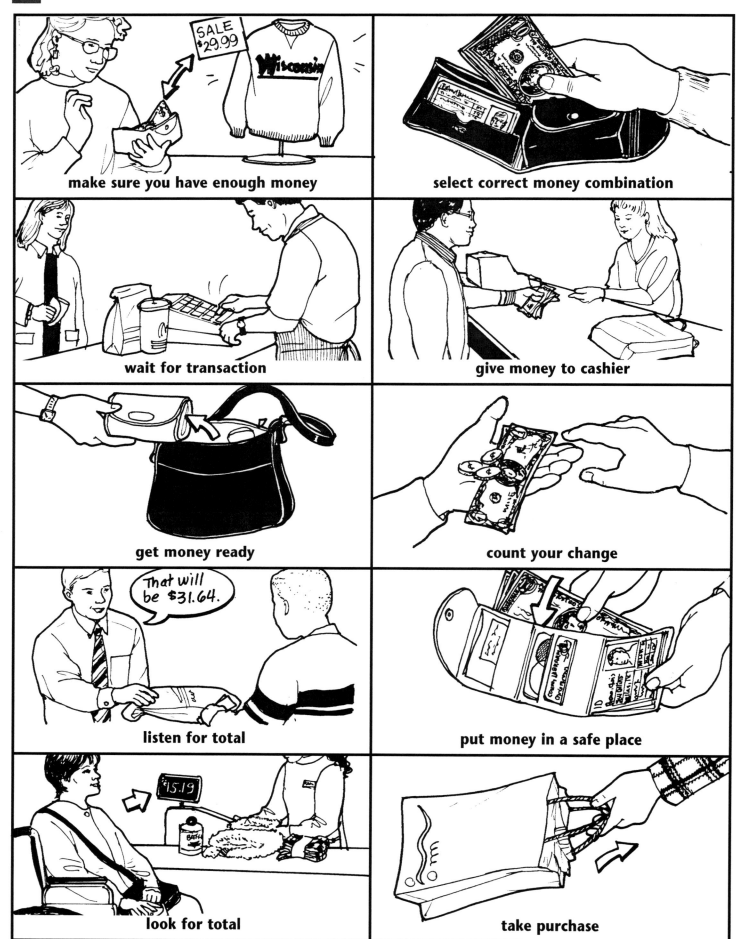

make sure you have enough money

select correct money combination

wait for transaction

give money to cashier

get money ready

count your change

listen for total

put money in a safe place

look for total

take purchase

ask if checks are accepted

write amount in words

carry ID/credit card

sign check

know amount of purchase

give check and show ID to cashier

write date and name

wait for receipt

write amount in numbers

record check and balance account

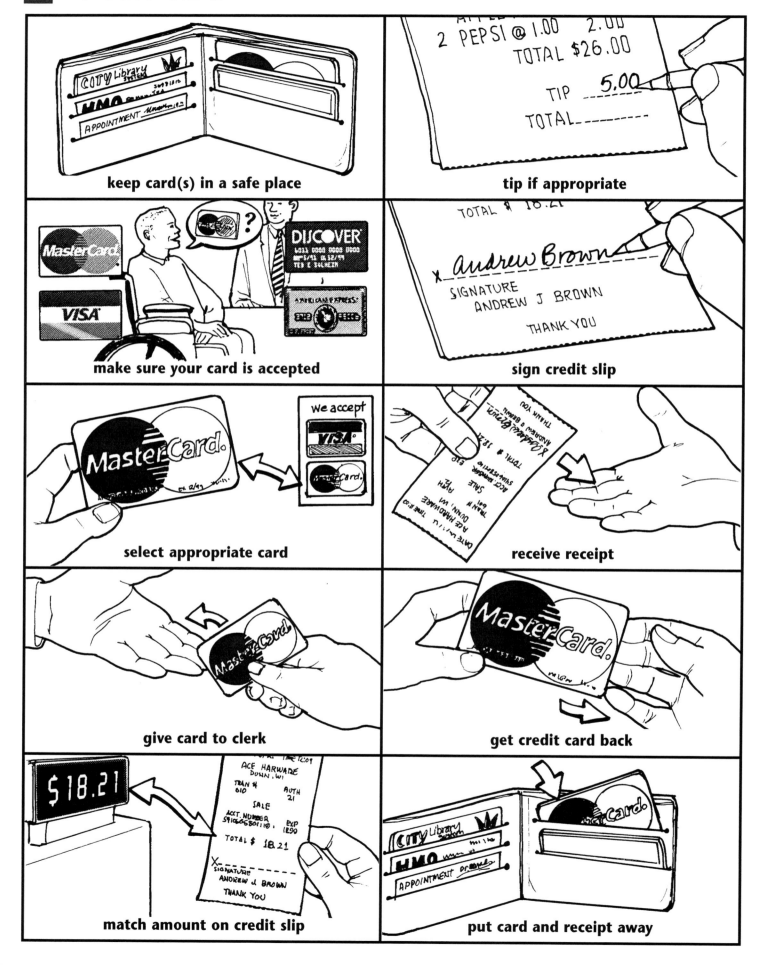

keep card(s) in a safe place

tip if appropriate

make sure your card is accepted

sign credit slip

select appropriate card

receive receipt

give card to clerk

get credit card back

match amount on credit slip

put card and receipt away

Social Skills: Automatic Teller Machine (ATM)

Wait patiently for your turn.

Give others personal space.

Keep receipts so no one can steal from your account.

Contact your bank right away if you don't get your card or money back.

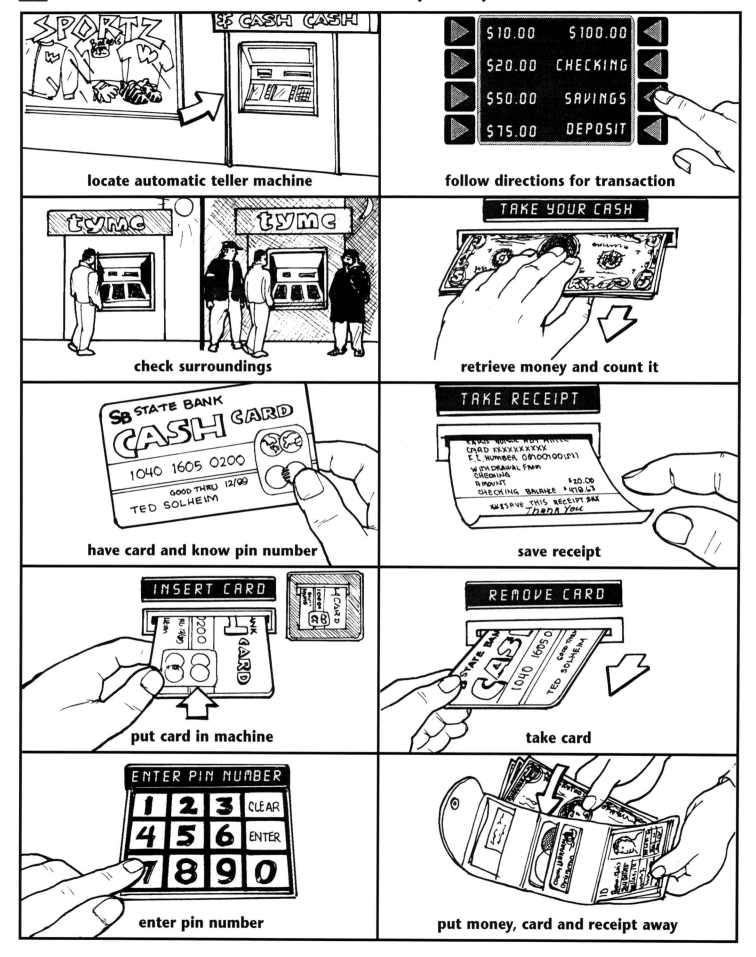

locate automatic teller machine

follow directions for transaction

check surroundings

retrieve money and count it

have card and know pin number

save receipt

put card in machine

take card

enter pin number

put money, card and receipt away

Potpourri

Community SUCCESS

Activity List

Social Skills: Library
Library
Social Skills: Post Office
Post Office
Social Skills: Voting
Voting
Social Skills: Laundromat
Laundromat

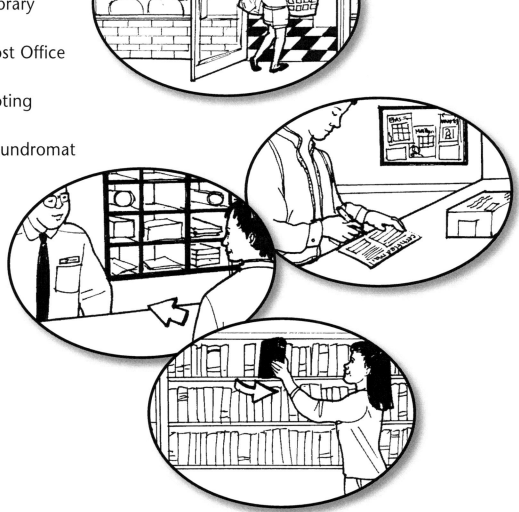

Social Skills: **Library**

When you make noise, you disturb others.

Learn where different items are located.

You pay a fine if materials are late — check the due dates!

If you don't pay your fines, you can't check out materials.

Social Skills: **Library**

Always return books to the same place after you look at them.

The librarians can help you — just ask.

At home, treat materials gently and with clean hands.

Always return materials to the return counter or drop box.

enter library

use computer (card catalog)

go to information desk if needed

locate material area

apply for library card

go to specific stack

know author's name and book title if possible

follow call number and alphabetical order

use card catalog

remove needed book from stack

Library

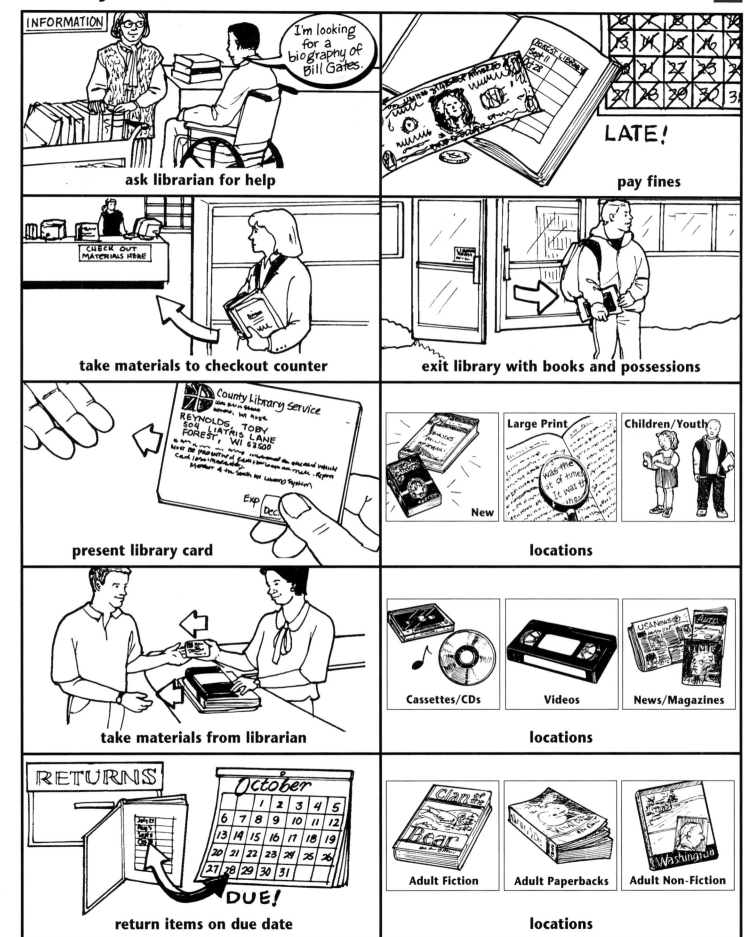

ask librarian for help

pay fines

take materials to checkout counter

exit library with books and possessions

present library card

locations

take materials from librarian

locations

return items on due date

locations

Social Skills: **Post Office**

Wait patiently in line.

Know when the post office is open.

Learn how to correctly prepare items to mail.

Address mail clearly with all necessary information.

address package or envelope

pick up mail

enter post office

type of mail   **choose how to mail**

EXPRESS MAIL
1st CLASS
PRIORITY MAIL
3rd CLASS
PARCEL POST

fill out necessary forms

select stamps

wait in line

pay for postage

go to counter

exit post office

Social Skills: Voting

Follow directions.

Keep your vote private.

Don't wear political buttons or clothing to the polls.

Take a list if you need help remembering your candidates.

Voting

register or pick up an absentee ballot

enter and close door/drapes

enter polling place

cast your vote/exit voting booth

wait in correct line (precinct or school district)

put ballot in voting machine or ballot box

give I.D. to poll worker — get number or ballot

exit polling place

go to empty booth or machine — give number

Voting location _____

Date _____ Hours _____

Precinct number ____ School district _____

My candidates _____

_____

_____

Social Skills: Laundromat

Keep your money and possessions close to you.

Watch your laundry so it isn't unattended.

Don't take up too much space.

Some days or times are not as busy.

Laundromat

sort laundry into basket(s)

find empty washer(s)

take detergent and laundry products

get tokens or change

take money

purchase laundry products

enter laundry

put laundry in washer(s)

select a place to sit

select washer setting

Laundromat

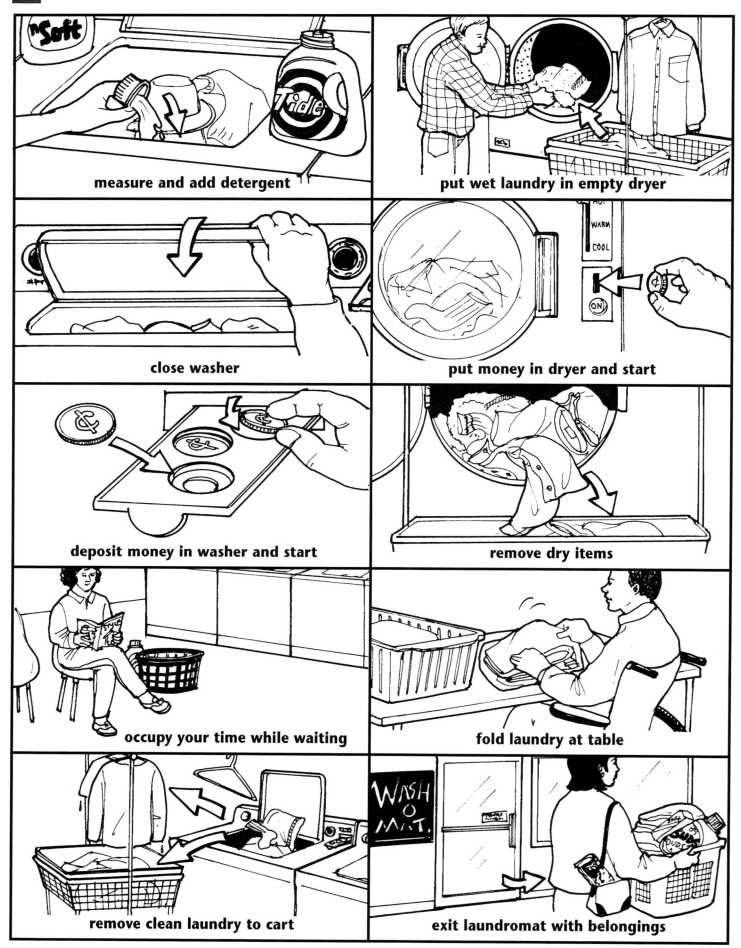

measure and add detergent

put wet laundry in empty dryer

close washer

put money in dryer and start

deposit money in washer and start

remove dry items

occupy your time while waiting

fold laundry at table

remove clean laundry to cart

exit laundromat with belongings

Appendix

Data Sheets

Community Success Progress Report

Activity Assessment Sheet

Activity Goals

Routine Goals

Community Success Progress Report

Student:

Helper:

Activities At Home	Date	Rating	Date	Rating	Date	Rating
1. Ready to Go						
2. Answering the Door						
3. Checking the House						
4. Coming Home						
Any Place						
5. Restroom Use						
6. Waiting in Line						
7. Asking for Help						
8. Crossing Streets						
9. Walking						
10. Wheelchair Travel						
11. Elevator						
12. Escalator						
Going Places						
13. Packing						
14. Vacation						
15. Hotel-Motel						
16. Car						
17. Gas Station						
18. Bus						
19. Bicycle						
20. Taxi						

Activities	Date	Rating	Date	Rating	Date	Rating
21. Airplane						
22. Commuter Train						
23. Grocery Shopping						
24. Dept. Store						
25. Clothing Purchase						
26. Pharmacy						
27. Vending Machine						
Eating Out						
28. Fast Food						
28. Pizza Delivery						
30. Table Service						
31. Buffet						
32. Cafeteria						
33. Dinner Invitation						
Appointments						
34. Telephone Appt.						
35. Waiting Room						
36. Doctor						
37. Dentist						
38. Eye Exam						
39. Veterinarian						
40. Hair Care						

Activities Money Matters	Date	Rating	Date	Rating	Date	Rating
41. Bank						
42. Cash Purchases						
43. Check Writing						
44. Credit Card						
45. Automatic Teller						
Potpourri						
46. Library						
47. Post Office						
48. Voting						
49. Laundromat						

Rating Key: ⊞ can do independently   ⊟ in training   ☒ can't perform the activity but not in training   ☐ not applicable

Activity Assessment Sheet

Activity: _____ Student: _____

Location:	Date	Date	Date	Date	Date
Steps:					
1.					
2.					
3.					
4.					
5.					
6.					
7.					
8.					
9.					
10.					
11.					
12.					
13.					
14.					
15.					
16.					

Rating Key: ⊞ well done   ⊟ poorly done   ⊠ did not do   ☐ not applicable

Comments: _____
_____
_____
_____
_____
_____
_____
_____
_____

Goal set: _____ (date)   **Review:** _____ (date)

Activity Goals

Statement 1.   Date _____

_____ will learn to _____

name

by _____. Success is defined by completing _____ out of _____ steps.

date

Presently, s/he can do _____ step correctly. Training will occur in these locations:

_____.

Prompts to be given are: _____

_____.

Special conditions include: _____.

Statement 2.   Date _____

_____ will _____

name

by _____. Success is defined by completing _____ out of _____ steps.

date

Presently, s/he can do _____ step correctly. The student (will) (will not) refer to picture cues.

S/he will receive no prompts from the instructor during this activity. It will take no longer than _____

minutes: seconds

to complete and will be successfully performed on _____ occasions in these locations:

_____.

Special conditions include: _____.

Routine Goals

Statement 1.   Date _____

_____ will be able to do these activities correctly and in sequence by
          name

_____ : _____, _____, _____,
   date

_____ : _____, _____, _____,

S/he (will) (will not) refer to picture cues. Prompts to be given are: _____

_____.   The routine will be practiced in these locations:

_____.

Special conditions include: _____.

Statement 2.   Date _____

_____ will be able to do these activities correctly in sequence by
          name

_____ : _____, _____, _____,
   date

_____ : _____, _____, _____,

S/he (will) (will not) refer to picture cues. The instructor will give no prompts and the routine will be completed

within _____, _____ times consecutively. The routine will be practiced in
      minutes: seconds

these locations: _____.

Special conditions are: _____.